The Financial Times Guide to Business Numeracy

How to check the figures for yourself

Second edition

Leo Gough

Financial Times
Prentice Hall
is an imprint of

Harlow, England • London • New York • Boston • San Francisco • Toronto • Sydney • Singapore • Hong Kong
Tokyo • Seoul • Taipei • New Delhi • Cape Town • Madrid • Mexico City • Amsterdam • Munich • Paris • Milan

PEARSON EDUCATION LIMITED

Edinburgh Gate
Harlow CM20 2JE
Tel: +44 (0)1279 623623
Fax: +44 (0)1279 431059
Website: www.pearson.com/uk

First edition published in 1994
Second edition published in Great Britain in 2011

© Pearson Education Limited 1994, 2011

The right of Leo Gough to be identified as author of this work has been asserted
by him in accordance with the Copyright, Designs and Patents Act 1988.

Pearson Education is not responsible for the content of third-party internet sites.

ISBN: 978-0-273-74643-0

British Library Cataloguing-in-Publication Data
A catalogue record for this book is available from the British Library

Library of Congress Cataloging-in-Publication Data
Gough, Leo.
  The Financial times guide to business numeracy : how to check the figures for yourself / Leo
Gough. -- 2nd ed.
    p. cm.
  Includes index.
  ISBN 978-0-273-74643-0 (pbk.)
  1. Business mathematics. I. Financial times (London, England) II. Title. III. Title: Guide to
business numeracy.

  HF5691.G68 2011
  650.01'513--dc23

                    2011033609

10 9 8 7 6 5 4 3 2 1
15 14 13 12 11

Typeset in 9pt Stone Serif by 30
Printed by Ashford Colour Press Ltd, Gosport

Contents

Preface

How often have you been at a meeting where someone is pushing you to agree to a proposal based on their figures alone? How often have you listened to predictions of imminent disaster, based on someone else's analysis of anything from the MMR vaccine to the world financial crisis?

We all know that we shouldn't accept every figure we are given on trust. Politicians, the media, suppliers, customers, and even people in our own organisations, may have strong incentives to quote misleading figures. Even if they are not doing so deliberately, people often misguidedly choose the figures that present their case in the best light, rather than to provide an objective view. And sometimes, people just make mistakes. Checking the figures helps you not only to avoid costly mistakes, but also to optimise the outcomes of your decisions.

This book aims to provide you with the basic tools you need to check other people's figures, either directly by reproducing their calculations, or by using alternative methods that may be more valid. Often, just checking the assumptions of the analysis is enough to identify glaring sources of error or bias. We look at commonly occurring issues, such as how to:

- deal with uncertainty;
- examine assumptions;
- assess the validity of surveys and polls;
- spot misleading statements;
- think critically about what the data really tell you;
- check estimates, forecasts and projections;
- make informed investment decisions;
- optimise outcomes in complex projects.

Even if you were put off by mathematics at school, you still need understandable, usable mathematical tools to solve business problems, from the stock market to public relations, from warehousing to the corner shop. And, increasingly, we are all expected to have a basic understanding of concepts such as indexing because of the role they play in interpreting economic trends. For instance, if someone tells you that the Consumer Price Index was rebased in 2005, most managers would be expected to know what that means. This book tries to make the link between the abstractions of mathematics and its practical application in business, using clear, real-life examples.

To illustrate the power of checking the numbers for yourself, here's an example how an outsider was able to challenge the figures given by a major multinational by making some basic calculations of his own.

Real-life stories   **Oil flow in the Gulf of Mexico**

After the Gulf of Mexico oil spill began on 20 April 2010, for several weeks BP estimated the amount of oil flowing into the sea at 5,000 barrels a day. In the absence of other estimates, this figure was widely reported in the world's media. Then BP released video footage of the plume of oil escaping into the sea. An engineering professor, Steve Wereley, analysed the footage frame by frame to estimate the rate of flow (he came up with 2 feet per second), and then used a simple formula to calculate the volume of a cylinder:

$$v = \pi r^2 h$$

where v is the volume, r is the radius of the cylinder and h is the height or length of cylinder.

Of course, as the oil flows into the sea it doesn't maintain a cylinder shape and disperses into a shapeless mass, but the volume of oil in this mass is the same as if it were a cylinder, so it is appropriate to use the formula.

Wereley's estimate was much higher than BP's estimate of 5,000 barrels a day. He reckoned that the flow was about 70,000 barrels a day, plus or minus 20%, with an additional 20,000 barrels a day from other, smaller leaks. This new, much larger estimate was used by the US government to bring pressure on BP to act more decisively to plug the leak, and was reported in the media as the result of very detailed scientific analysis.

Well, yes, it was the result of detailed scientific analysis, but it was the kind of analysis that anyone with a basic knowledge of physics and geometry could have performed without any very fancy machinery or software.

The moral of the story? It is often possible for you to check the accuracy of other people's figures by making your own calculations. Your sums don't necessarily have to produce precise results: as long as you make a good estimate of the margin of error, if your results are markedly different from the other person's figures, you have good grounds to ask some very searching questions.

- **Chapters 1 and 2** provide an introduction to the basic concepts and techniques of statistical research and how they are applied in business.
- **Chapter 3** looks at good and bad ways of presenting information using charts and tables.
- **Chapter 4** deals with the art and science of forecasting, looking in detail at time series, regression analysis and reference class forecasting.
- **Chapter 5** examines several specialised decision-making techniques, game theory, Markov chains, network analysis and queueing.
- **Chapter 6** looks at the key concepts in finance and investment, including interest, inflation, discounted cashflow and indexing.
- **Chapter 7** examines theories and investment techniques used in the stock market and discusses their effectiveness.
- **Chapter 8** looks at probability, which is the foundation of many analytical and statistical decision-making methods.
- **The Appendix** provides a refresher in mathematic notation and some basic concepts, including percentages, factorials, rounding, significant figures and logarithms.
- **The Glossary** contains some essential terms for quick reference.

In business, you can never be too numerate. After working through this book you should have a basic understanding of the principal mathematical methods used in business which you can then develop through further study if you wish.

1

Dealing with large amounts of information: how to summarise and describe it

All organisations depend on large quantities of information – or 'data' – to function. These collections of data may be generated internally – relating to products, inventories and customers, for example – or they may be produced externally by, for example, trade organisations and government departments, and relate to larger populations, such as an entire industry or a country.

Many day-to-day decisions, and most medium to long-term decisions, rely heavily on these numbers. Clearly, this information needs to be collected and analysed as accurately as possible in order to make the best decisions, but, as we will see throughout this book, for a number of reasons there are a lot of inaccurate, misleading and downright false data out there. The present chapter focuses on the basics of getting and handling data accurately, but we also need to develop skills to assess the quality of the data analyses that we use (see Chapter 2).

In this chapter we will look at how to summarise and describe large quantities of data using basic methods that you probably learned at school; applied properly, these methods are very powerful, and it is surprising how often business people just don't make full of use them. For instance, if you don't know, or have forgotten, what a 'standard deviation' is, you should definitely read this chapter.

Why do data matter?

Information is at the heart of business, and while you may be able avoid dealing with it and still hold down a job, you will never become a successful decision-maker until you can make sense of data. This usually involves being able to deal with summaries of data rapidly, by reading, understanding and interpreting them. Here are just a few examples of how useful data can be in making business decisions:

■ You are a manager of a small supermarket chain, and you want to optimise the mix of products that you sell in your stores, which is constantly changing according to season and trends in consumer demand. Using raw data collected at the checkout counters by scanning the bar codes of every product sold, you can analyse them to monitor the changes constantly, spot trends, control stock levels, identify new customer buying patterns and plan for the introduction of new products. Suppose, for instance, a local supplier offers you a new kind of game pie; using your sales data analysis, you can identify which of your stores are likely to be able to move the product, where the product should be in the store, and which kind of customer is likely to buy the product. After a trial period, you can analyse whether your hypothesis was correct: did the product sell as you expected, for instance? If the results warrant it, you can then run further trials to see if a different sales approach produces better results.

■ You are considering opening a large specialist designer kitchen store somewhere in the south-east of England. Which town should you choose, and where in the town should you site your store? Before coming to a decision there are many points you will have to consider, including how many of your potential customers might actually come to your shop in a given location. The answer to this question will almost certainly not be available on a plate: you'll have to be creative in acquiring sources of data that might help you to reach a reasonably accurate estimate. For example, it would be helpful to know the current sales figures for designer kitchens in the area, how many people who could afford a designer kitchen live in the area, where they live, and whether they are likely to buy a designer kitchen next year. Some of these data could be obtained from external sources, but you would almost certainly also have to conduct some market research of your own, by contacting a representative sample of your target customers to discover much more about what they want, and how they make their decision to buy. The point here is that no single set of data or analytical method is likely to produce a complete and definitive answer to your question: you will have to conduct a series of different tests in order to build up a body of evidence upon which to base your final decision.

■ You are a management consultant hired by a large international firm to advise on its salary policy worldwide. You'll need access to a vast amount of information on what it currently pays its employees, what it used to pay, and what it expects to pay in the future. In order to produce meaningful recommendations, you'll need to analyse these data comprehensively, broken down by many different categories, such as region and job type, and compare them with other information, such as performance, job satisfaction, and salary levels within the firm and within other comparable organisations.

■ A drug company has discovered a new medicine for treating a disease. Before bringing it to market, it must conduct extensive and rigorous trials, often lasting more than a decade, to ensure that the potential benefits of the medicine outweigh the drawbacks. In general, the larger the number of patients in the trials, the better the measurement of the effects of the drug. If even only a small number of patients suffer bad side effects from the drug, this may be sufficient for the regulators to refuse permission to sell the drug. In the past, when the rules on testing were less strict, tragedies occurred, such as the thalidomide case of the late 1950s and early 1960s, where a large number of pregnant mothers who were given thalidomide to prevent morning sickness subsequently had babies with physical malformations. Although the manufacturers and licensees had tested thalidomide before selling it, they had not done this as rigorously and extensively as is required today. It took several years before an Australian gynaecologist, W.G. McBride, alerted medics to the problem in a letter in *The Lancet*, noting that while birth defects were normally 1.5% of all babies, he was finding in his own practice that almost 20% of his pregnant patients who had taken thalidomide were giving birth to babies with abnormalities.[1]

Summarising large quantities of data

If you can summarise a set of data simply, you can describe it, and use it to make high-level statements and comparisons that may be sufficient for your purposes. For example, if you can summarise the sales data for a rock concert you organised last year by saying 'the majority of our customers

---

[1] McBride, W.G. (1961) 'Thalidomide and congenital abnormalities', *Lancet,* 2:1358.

spent between £5 and £15 each on food and drink', this may be all you need to know for the time being, and it leaves the door open for more detailed and sophisticated analysis of the data should you need to answer more detailed questions about your customers' spending later. Often, though, all you need is a straightforward summary to make your point.

There are three main ways to summarise data:

1 You can give a 'typical' value. For example, 'our customers typically spent between £5 and £15 each on food and drink'.

2 You can give a figure for the 'dispersion', or 'spread', of the figures in your set of data. For example, you could continue the description above by saying, 'individual customers spent between £0 and £50'.

3 You can describe the 'distribution', or pattern of the data. In our example of the rock concert, if 20% of our customers spent nothing on food and drink, 70% spent between £5 and £15, 7% spent between £15 and £50, and 3% spent over £50 each, you could say that the pattern of spending was 'right-skewed' or 'positively skewed', meaning that there were far more customers in the £0–£15 range (see Figure 1.1).

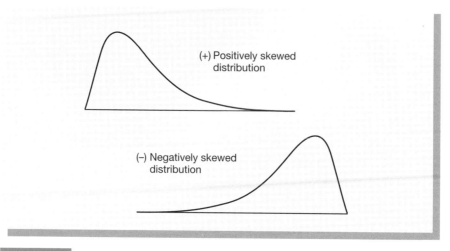

Figure 1.1   Skewed distributions

Taken together, these three ways of summarising data enable us to give a succinct description of a dataset. In practice, however, simply giving a 'typical' value is often sufficient. In the next section we'll look at the three most commonly used methods of measuring a typical value, which are kinds of average.

Summarising data 1: averages – a refresher

Averages express the middle point in a set of numbers (or 'observations'). There are three principle ways to calculate an average. Each method produces a number with a different meaning, so when you are presented with an average, you should always check how it was calculated.

The arithmetic mean

This is the most commonly used average. To calculate it, add together all the numbers in the set and divide by the number of observations in the set.

Example

You have six regular customers for a product. You know how much each one has spent. You want to find the mean average spent.

Step 1. Add the amounts together.

Customer 1	25,001
Customer 2	34,340
Customer 3	100
Customer 4	25,003
Customer 5	100
Customer 6	112,890
Total	197,434

Step 2. Divide the total by the number of customers.

$$197,434 \div 6 = 32,905.66$$

The mean average that your customers spent is £32,905.66.

That's easy, but the trouble with this figure is that it might give you the impression that most of your customers spend around £32,905.66. In fact, the majority spent considerably less than this, and it was one big spender, Customer 6, who brought the mean average up. Technically, this property of the mean can be described as a susceptibility to the influence of outlying observations that are much larger or smaller than the majority of the observations. The distribution of the data is negatively skewed because of Customer 6. In such circumstances, using a different way of calculating averages may be more helpful, such as the median.

The median

The median gives the middle point in a set of observations. This is useful for describing a typical value for a skewed distribution. Calculate the median by ranking the numbers (observations) in order of value and take the middle number. If there is an even number of observations, add the two observations in the middle and divide by half.

Example

Step 1. Using the same observations as in the previous example, rank your customers by how much they spent:

Customer 3	100
Customer 5	100
Customer 1	25,001
Customer 4	25,003
Customer 2	34,340
Customer 6	112,890

Step 2. Add the two middle numbers in the series, Customer 1 and Customer 4:

Customer 1	25,001
Customer 4	25,003
Total	50,004

Step 3. Divide the total by 2.

$$50,004 \div 2 = 25,002$$

The median is £25,002.

This result tells you that half of your customers spent more than £25,002 and half your customers spent less. In this example, the median gives a better idea of the average spend than the mean average of £32,905.66, since all but one of the customers spent less than the mean.

Reminder: if there is an odd number of observations, take the middle one, and if there is an even number of observations, take the middle two and divide by two. When there are more than about 30 observations, you don't usually need to take the middle two and divide by two because the difference will usually be too small to matter.

Real-life stories   **The median in real life**

The median is generally used for reporting skewed distributions like average incomes and house prices. These are, of course, hot political issues, and politicians and NGOs often say very odd things about them. For example, in the UK, both Labour and Conservative politicians talk a lot about 'relative poverty', defined as those whose incomes are below a certain percentage (usually 60%) of the median income. That's fine, until people start dropping the word 'relative'. The median income in 2010 was about £23,000, so that would mean that anyone earning less than £13,800 was 'relatively poor'. But if you earned, say, £13,000 would you necessarily be very 'poor'? What if you were 18 years old and living with your parents, for instance? In that case, £13,000 might be sufficient to have quite a nice life, allowing you to pay for plenty of clothes, boozy weekends and cheap foreign holidays. The point here, as is so often the case, that we need more information before we jump to any conclusions – the 18-year-old earning £13,000 a year may have a higher disposable income than, say, someone with a big mortgage who is earning substantially more.

The mode

The mode tells you the most commonly appearing, or 'popular', number in a set of observations.

Example

Using the same example, list your customers:

Customer 3	100
Customer 5	100
Customer 1	25,001
Customer 4	25,003
Customer 2	34,340
Customer 6	112,890

Customers 3 and 5 both spent £100, so the mode (the most commonly appearing number) is £100. Sometimes a series of observations has more than one mode. The series (5, 7, 8, 8, 8, 9, 11, 15, 16, 16, 16, 21, 21, 21) has three modes: 8, 16 and 21.

Modes are more useful with large numbers of observations, in particular, when you want to say something about mutually exclusive categories (known as 'categorical data'). Suppose you want to know the most popular way of getting work:

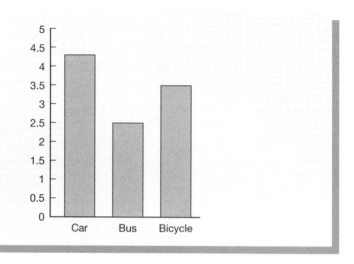

Figure 1.2   **Methods of going to work**

In this case, travel by car is the modal average, and is the correct answer. It would be meaningless to attempt to add together the numbers in the different categories and divide by three to obtain the mean average.

Test yourself: Part 1

Look at Table 1.1 below and answer the statements 'yes' or 'no'.

Table 1.1 Percentage of customers purchasing selected items

Age	Books	Magazines	Newspapers
15–19	14.6	16.1	33.5
20–24	20	27.4	68.7
25–29	25.6	25.3	70.9
30–34	18.5	17.4	69.5
35–39	14.2	8.1	62.9
40–44	10	4.3	62.7
Average	17.3	16	61.9

1 10% of customers who bought books were aged 40–44.

2 10% of customers aged 40–44 bought books.

3 Customers aged 40–44 were twice as likely to buy books as those aged 20–24.

See page 203 for the answers.

The weighted average and the geometric mean

There are two other kinds of average that you are likely to encounter, for example in information about investments: the weighted average and the geometric mean.

The weighted average usually refers to the 'weighted average mean', but sometimes other averages are weighted, so it's worth checking to make sure which average is being used. The 30 companies that are the components of the Dow Jones Industrial Average, a famous stock market index, for example, are weighted by price, so a company whose shares cost $200 each is given 10 times more weight than a company whose shares cost $20.

Example

You sell three washing machines for every one dryer in your store. The profit on washing machines is £150 each and the profit on dryers is £125. What's the weighted average profit of each item you sell?

Step 1. Identify the components (washers and dryers) and weight them according to the proportion sold. The weights should add up to 1.

Washers – 0.75

Dryers – 0.25

Step 2. Multiply the profit on each component by their weight and add the results together:

$$150 \times 0.75 = 112.5$$
$$125 \times 0.25 = 31.25$$
$$112.5 + 31.25 = 143.75$$

The weighted average profit on items sold is £143.75

Calculating the weighted average can be a bit tricky, and is discussed further on page 139.

The geometric mean is used in situations involving growth over time.

Example

Suppose your firm's sales figures are as follows:

Growth in sales		
Year 1	100	
Year 2	180	80%
Year 3	210	16.7%
Year 4	300	42.9%

You could calculate the mean average of the growth as (80% + 16.7% + 42.9%) ÷ 3 = 46.5%.

But look at what happens if you try to multiply 100 over 3 years by 46.5%:

$$\text{Year 2 } 100 + (100 \times 0.465) = 146.5$$

$$\text{Year 3 } 146.5 + (146.5 \times 0.465) = 146.5 + 68.12 = 214.62$$

$$\text{Year 4 } 214.62 + (214.62 \times 0.465) = 214.62 + 99.80 = 314.42$$

If you calculate the mean average of the growth rate in the normal way (known as the 'linear average'), by year 4 you get 314.42, not 300. This method overstates the growth rate.

That's why we use the geometric mean. You do this by multiplying the growth rates of years 2–4 together and taking the cube root (because there are three of them):

$$(1.8 \times 1.167 \times 1.429)^{\frac{1}{3}} = 1.443$$

Note that for the growth rates of each year we use 1.8, not 0.8, and so on, in this calculation.

If you now multiply 100 over 3 years by 44.3%, you will get the correct final total, which is 300.

Spotting errors and deliberate mistakes with averages

All of us are constantly bombarded with claims based on statistical information, many of which are incorrect, either from ignorance or from a deliberate intention to deceive. Some journalists seem to spend most of their time rewriting statistics from government handouts, and then either get them wrong or draw the wrong conclusions from them. If the article notes the title of the report and where it can be obtained, at least you can check it for yourself, but often this information is absent, which is a good indicator of possible problems.

Here's a trick some kids use to explain to their parents that they don't have any time to go to school:

There are 365 days in the year. A third of the time is spent sleeping, which is a total of 122 days, leaving 243 days. Three hours a day are spent having meals, totalling approximately 45 days.

$$243 - 45 = 198$$

The summer holidays are 90 days a year, which leaves 108 days. Christmas and Easter take up another 21 days, leaving 87 days. There are 52 weekends a year, totalling 104 days, so the result is a minus number. Therefore, there can't possibly be any time available for going to school.

Q Can you spot what's wrong with this argument?

See page 203 for the answer.

Averages are among the most frequently abused figures. We have seen that they are often very different values; the fact that they can all be called 'the average' offers enormous scope for misrepresentation. Consider the following statement:

'The median age of software entrepreneurs is 37 and their average income is £42,000.'

Does this mean that the median income is £42,000? We don't know, and unless it is stated elsewhere in the text, there is no way of finding out without seeing the raw data. Suppose that the person who wrote this statement was unscrupulously trying to make the average income as big as possible and the average age as small as possible, and that the medians of both were smaller than their arithmetic means. The median has been chosen for the first figure, to make it smaller, and the arithmetic mean has been chosen for the second, to make it look larger. We read 'the median age', and, unless we are careful, we assume that the average income is also the median.

The beauty of this kind of deception is that, even when exposed, the deceiver cannot actually be said to have made a false statement, merely an imprecise one.

Here's another sleight of hand done with averages. Suppose a company has three directors, who also own all its shares. They have 403 employees, including themselves, and are in the middle of a wage dispute. To bolster their arguments against increasing wages due insufficient profits, the directors produce the following figures:

Average salary	£23,000
Average profit to each shareholder	£20,000

The average used is the arithmetic mean. Suppose that the total wage bill of the 400 employees (not counting the directors) is £7,200,000. This gives a mean wage of £18,000 per employee, so how have they arrived at the figure of £23,000? We can work this out:

$$\text{Mean of 400 salaries 18,000}$$
$$\text{Mean of 403 salaries} = 23,000$$
$$(7,200,000 + x) \div 403 = 23,000$$
$$7,200,000 + x = 9,269,000$$
$$x = 2,069,000$$

The value for x is the total of the three directors' salaries; while their average profit is £20,000 each, their average salary is 2,069,000 + 3 = £689,667. Thus, the figures could be written as:

$$\text{Average salary of non-shareholding employees} = £18,000$$

$$\text{Average salary and profit of owner/directors} = £709,667$$

which, from the directors' point of view, spoils the argument. In effect, the directors are taking most of the profits as salaries. This is a crude example which could probably be spotted quite easily by the employees, but might well be hard to catch when interwoven with more complex arguments.

Summarising data 2: dispersion

Averages, remember, give a 'typical' value for a set of data, which is useful. It can be made even more useful if you also have a figure for the 'dispersion', or 'spread', of the figures in your set of data. For example, if someone tells you that in a certain seaside resort hotel rooms cost £30 a night on average, they give a clearer picture if they add that prices in the resort range from £5 to £35 – this suggests that most of the hotels in the resort are at the higher end of the range.

Quantiles: quartiles, deciles and percentiles

A good way to give more information about dispersion is to chop up the data into parts, or 'quantiles'. Often, a set of data is divided into four roughly equal parts, using three 'quartile' values, or 10 roughly equal parts, giving 'decile' values, or 100 roughly equal parts, giving 'percentile values'.

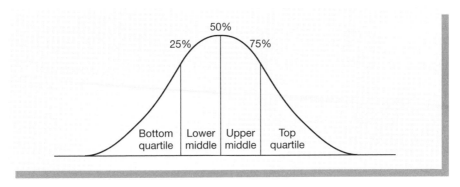

50%

25%   75%

| Bottom quartile | Lower middle | Upper middle | Top quartile |

Figure 1.3   Quartiles

Figure 1.3   Quartiles

Figure 1.3 shows a set of data that has been divided into four. Notice that the three vertical red lines that divide the data into four are the quartile cut-off points. The term 'quartile' has two meanings. It can refer to one of the four subsets of data – so if you say 'my TV show was in the top quartile of viewing figures', it means that your TV show was in the top 25% of viewing figures for TV shows. Secondly, it can refer to one of the cut-off points – so if you talk about the 'upper quartile' (sometimes marked Q3 or UQ) you may be talking only about the value at the third vertical line in Figure 1.3. There are several ways to calculate the quartile cut-off values, too. You can choose values from the data points that you have, or you can choose ones that fall between the data points – but in the latter case, there are at least five different ways to calculate the cut-off values.

Quantiles are easy to understand in principle, but can be very confusing to calculate in practice, and you should be aware that computer programs vary a lot in the calculation methods they use. For general business purposes, however, these distinctions don't usually make much difference.

The range and the semi-interquartile

The 'range' is the difference between the highest and lowest numbers in a set of numbers. For example, the range of (3, 5, 6, 7, 9, 11, 23, 145) is 145 – 3 = 142. The trouble with this is that the highest number, 145, is so extreme and thus distorts the range. To deal with this, we can carve up the set into quarters, tenths or hundredths.

To prevent the distortion created by an extreme value, or 'outlier', we can ignore the first and last quarters of the set of observations and calculate the range between the first quartile and third quartile, the middle 50% of the set. This is called the 'semi-interquartile', or 'interquartile' range (IQR) which is simply the range between the first and third cut-off points (the vertical lines on the left and right in Figure 1.3). The IQR is not affected by extreme values, and gives a good description of the middle 50% of the data.

Example

Consider the collection of numbers (3, 5, 6, 7, 9, 11, 23, 145). The first quarter includes 3 and 5. The first quartile, or Q1, is the average of the last number of the first quarter and the first number of the second; (5 + 6) ÷ 2 = 5.5. In the same way, we can calculate the second quartile Q2 as (7 + 9) ± 2 = 8 and Q3 as (11 + 23) ± 2 = 17. The semi-interquartile range is from Q2 to Q3, so is the interval (5.5, 17). Notice that Q2 is the median.

Standard deviation

A more conceptually difficult, but also more powerful, tool for describing dispersion is 'standard deviation'. The standard deviation is calculated in a similar way to the arithmetic mean; it is basically the mean of the deviations of each observation from the mean. Doing this by hand is long-winded, but most computer spreadsheets and scientific calculators will do it for you. Among other things, standard deviation is a very useful statistical method for estimating the variability we can expect in the future.

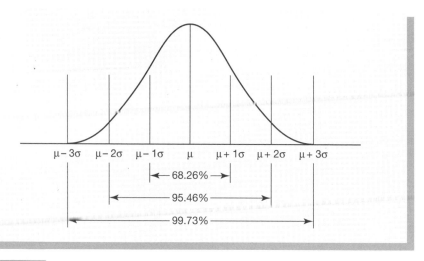

Figure 1.4   Standard deviations in a normal distribution

In 'normal distributions' (see page 17), roughly 68% of a distribution is contained within one standard deviation either side of the mean, roughly 95% within two standard deviations, and 99.73% within three standard deviations. Figure 1.4 illustrates this, using the symbols σ ('sigma') for the standard deviation and μ ('mu') for the mean. As you can see, the standard deviation shows you how closely (or loosely) your data are bunched around the mean; in Figure 1.4 we see a pattern of dispersion (normal distribution) that is common in nature (we'll return to this point a little later). For example, people's IQs have a normal distribution, the average IQ is set at 100, and the standard distribution is found to be 15; this tells us that roughly 68% of people have an IQ within the range of 85 and 115 (from 100 − 15 = 85 to 100 + 15 = 115).

Example

Imagine that you have two salespeople who have been selling a product for a year, and that both salespeople have sold an average £70,000 worth of goods each week. Calculating the standard deviation for Salesperson A, you find that it is 3,000, while Salesperson B's standard deviation is 5,000. This shows that Salesperson B's results vary more widely than Salesperson A's. You can predict that if other factors remain constant, about 68% of Salesperson A's weekly figures in the future will be between 67,000 and 73,000 and that 68% of Salesperson B's figures will be between 65,000 and 75,000.

Calculating the standard deviation

You can work out the standard deviation on most scientific calculators by adding the observations and pressing the σx key. It's quite tiresome to work out by hand, but just so that you know the principle, here's how to do it:

Step 1. You have the set (6, 8, 10, 12). What's the standard deviation? First, calculate the mean:

$$(6 + 8 + 10 + 12) \div 4 = 9.$$

Step 2. Calculate the deviation from the mean for each number:

$$6 - 9 = -3$$
$$8 - 9 = -1$$
$$10 - 9 = 1$$
$$12 - 9 = 3$$

Two of the deviations are minus numbers. Notice that if you add all the deviations together, the sum is zero. For this reason, the deviations are squared, which produces all positive numbers.

Step 3. Calculate the squares of each deviation:

$$-1 \times -1 = 1$$
$$-3 \times -3 = 9$$
$$1 \times 1 = 1$$
$$3 \times 3 = 9$$

Step 4. Add the squares together:

$$9 + 1 + 9 + 1 = 20.$$

Divide this by the number of observations, which is 4.

$$20 \div 4 = 5.$$

This result is called the 'variance'.

Step 5. To get the standard deviation, calculate the square root of the variance.

$$\sqrt{5} = 2.23.$$

Real-life stories   **Standard deviation in real life: Six Sigma**

In the 1980s a large telecommunications company, Motorola, developed a rigorous methodology for eliminating defects from its manufacturing processes. The idea was that even a relatively small number of defective products were actually costing the company a lot of money, substantially more than had been acknowledged earlier. The company aimed to make defect-free products six standard deviations from the mean, or 99.99966% of its output. The symbol for standard deviation being σ, or 'sigma', the methodology was christened 'Six Sigma'.

Many other major manufacturing firms adopted the approach; over the years it has been adapted to other business functions and industries and has now become a management training and consultancy industry in its own right. It's clearly best suited to large firms, where small inefficiencies can gradually build up into massive amounts of waste, and to complex industries where customers have come to expect no mistakes. For example, when people buy a PC, use a cashpoint machine, or receive hospital treatment, these days they insist upon perfect products and perfect service. Without the statistical methods used by Six Sigma and similar quality management approaches, firms could not achieve today's standards, which are much higher than they were, say, 50 years ago.

So why did they choose six standard deviations, and not another number? After all, demanding only 3.4 mistakes in every 1 million products seems an unnecessarily high target. In fact, in a normal distribution, 6σ actually corresponds to only 2 mistakes in every 1 billion, but practitioners say that, over the long term, production processes tend to deteriorate, so they allow for the possibility that the 6σ quality rate slides back over time to 4.5σ, which corresponds to 3.4 mistakes in every 1 million products. Either way, the target seems both impossibly high and entirely arbitrary, as many critics have observed. The point really seems to be that Six Sigma tries to make waste reduction efforts really co-ordinated and measurable, so that managers can quantify their progress and translate it accurately into monetary terms. Having a clearly defined target helps, even if you don't always reach it!

Summarising data 3: distribution

The last of the three main measures used to summarise and describe data sets is the 'distribution', or pattern of the data. When you have a lot of values in your set, you can often illustrate it visually with a curve on a graph, as we have seen. Frequently, but not always, the curve will have a bulge in the middle, where there are many values, and tails on the outside, where there are fewer values.

Normal distribution

In many circumstances, if you have produced a set of numbers that has been influenced by many small independent forces, they form the sym-metrical 'bell-shaped' curve in Figure 1.5. This is known as the normal curve or 'Gaussian' curve after its discoverer, Carl Gauss, who described it in 1809. You will very often find that data, if sufficiently large, will have a normal distribution. If you know the mean and the standard deviation, you can draw the normal curve; this is the principal reason why standard deviation is so widely used. The mathematics of the normal curve is sim-pler than that of other curves, and the results obtained often apply quite well to other distribution patterns too; this makes the normal distribution a very useful tool for making statistical estimates.

All kinds of measurements have a normal distribution, for example, peo-ple's height, weight, blood pressure and shoe size, small differences in the size of a manufactured item and the height of trees in a forest.

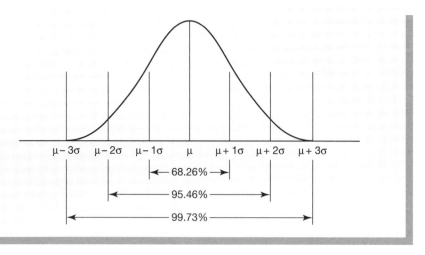

Figure 1.5   Normal distribution

Figure 1.5 shows the normal distribution again, that we saw in Figure 1.4 when discussing standard deviation. This time, let's focus on the main features of the normal distribution curve:

- The mean marks the mid-point of the curve.
- 50% of the distribution is on one side, and 50% on the other. The curve is symmetrical.
- Almost 100% of the distribution is within 3 standard deviations either side of the mid-point.
- 95% of the distribution is within 2 standard deviations either side of the mid-point.
- 68% of the distribution is within 1 standard deviation either side of the mid-point.

Example

Suppose you are the manager of a chain of bowling alleys. You hire out special bowling shoes to your customers, and you want to know how many of each size to keep in stock. Assuming that your customers' foot lengths are normally distributed, which is likely, and that you know that the mean is 11 inches in length and the standard deviation is 2, you can work out that:

3 standard deviations above the mean is 11 + 6 = 17.

3 standard deviations below the mean is 11 – 6 = 5.

Almost 100% of the bowling shoes must be between 5 and 17 inches long.

2 standard deviations above the mean is 11 + 4 = 15.

2 standard deviations below the mean is 11 − 4 = 7.

95% of the bowling shoes must be between 7 and 15 inches long.

1 standard deviation above the mean is 11 + 2 = 13.

1 standard deviation below the mean is 11 − 2 = 9.

68% of the bowling shoes must be between 9 and 13 inches.

You could use these figures to help plan your stock ordering. From these figures you might decide not to stock any bowling shoes outside the 7 to 15 inch range, and to keep about two-thirds of your stock in the 9 to 13 inch range.

Comparing two different distributions

It is quite common to come across two separate distributions that are comparable, but expressed in different units. To deal with this, calculate the standard deviation as a percentage of the mean for each distribution. The result is called the 'coefficient of variation'.

Example

Your British bowling alley company is buying a similar chain in Germany. You hope to cut the costs of buying bowling shoes through the combined purchasing power of the two chains. The mean of the German customers' foot lengths is 33 cm with a standard deviation of 3.

Step 1. Calculate the coefficient of variation of the British foot lengths by dividing the standard deviation by the mean.

$$(2 \div 11) \times 100 = 18.8\%.$$

Step 2. Calculate the coefficient of variation of the German foot lengths in the same way.

$$(3 \div 33) \times 100 = 9\%.$$

Step 3. Comparing these two results, you see that the spread of the British foot lengths (18.8%) is wider than the Germans' (9%); since the means of the two populations are nearly equivalent, you can see that in Germany you will need more shoes in the middle range of sizes and fewer in the more extreme ones,

Comparisons using z scores

Standard scores or 'z scores' are used to compare different measurements The z score equals the deviation score (the deviation of an observation from the mean), divided by the standard deviation, thus:

$$z = (x - \text{mean}) \div \text{standard deviation}$$

where x is any observation. A minus z score tells you that the observation is less than the mean, and a positive z score that it is greater than the mean.

If you convert all the observations in a distribution into z scores, you have 'standardised' the distribution. Tables for the normal distribution usually use this standardised form (see Table 1.2). At the mean, $z = 0$.

Table 1.2 Values for z, the standard normal variable, showing the probability that observations will lie between 0 and z

z	Probability
0	0
0.5	.192
1	.341
1.5	.433
1.96	.475
2	.477
2.5	.494
3	.499

Looking at Table 1.2, you can see that where $z = 1$, you get a reading of 0.341; this gives the percentage of the distribution enclosed between the mean and $z = 1$, which is, when rounded, 34%.

Doubling this figure, you get 68%, the population contained within 1 standard deviation either side of the mean. If you read off $z = 1.96$, the area enclosed is 0.475; double this to get 0.95, or 95%.

Example

Using the example of the chain of bowling alleys, suppose you want to know what proportion of customers have shoe sizes below 14 inches. You know that the standard deviation is 2 and the mean is 11, so the deviation score is 14 – 11 = 3.

$$z = \text{deviation score} \div \text{standard deviation } 3 \pm 2 = 1.5.$$

Reading from Table 1.2 we get 0.433, or 43.3%. Doubling this, we get 86.6% for the area between 8 and 14.

Looking at Figure 1.6, you can see that you still need to add the part of the distribution in the tail of the curve to the left of 8. Simply subtract the percentage of the
distribution between 14 and 8 from 100%:

$$100 - 86.6 = 13.4\%.$$

13.4% of the distribution is in the two tails.

Halving this, you get:

$$13.4 \div 2 = 6.7\%.$$

6.7 + 86.6 = 93.3%, which is the percentage of the distribution of shoe sizes below
14 inches. From this, you should be able to see that you can use the fact that the
normal curve is symmetrical to find out a good deal.

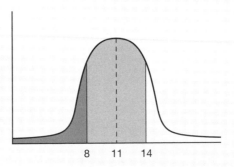

8   11   14

Figure 1.6   **Calculating sections of a distribution**

Other distributions

Although it is common to assume that any distribution you come across
is 'normal', it isn't always the case, and you should be aware that others
exist. For example, much of the behaviour of financial investments does
not follow a normal distribution (see Chapter 6). Another example of a
common 'non-normal' distribution is the random arrival of people
coming into a shop. These tend to form a 'Poisson distribution', which is
examined on page 119.

In the example of food sales at a rock concert on page 3, we noticed that the
distribution was 'skewed' – this tells us immediately that it is not a normal
distribution. Look back at the graphs of distributions in Figure 1.1. The distribution with the longer tail to the right has a positive skew, the one with the
longer tail to the left has a negative skew. You can use quartiles to discover

skew without drawing a graph; if (Q2 – Q1) > (Q3 – Q2), the skew is negative, and if (Q2 – Q1) < (Q3 – Q2) the skew is positive.

For example, imagine a survey of the distribution of a country's wealth amongst its people. Expressing this on a graph with the number of people on the vertical axis and the amount of wealth on the horizontal might show a distribution with positive skew (see Figure 1.7). If you had the observations, you could discover this skew, and hence the distribution shape, using the quartile method described above, so you would know, without drawing the graph, that many people had little wealth and a few people had a lot.

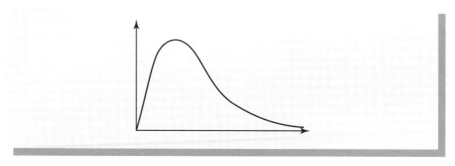

Figure 1.7   **Graph of wealth distribution (hypothetical)**

Real-life stories   **Skew in real life**

When someone who knows about statistics uses the expression 'skewed data', it does not mean that there is anything wrong with the data, or that the data have been deliberately distorted. It is just a descriptive remark about the distribution, telling us that it's not a normal distribution, and has some outlying values.

However, in the media and the blogosphere, you frequently encounter the expression 'skewed data' in a negative or moralistic sense. For instance, it may refer to a claim that data have been misinterpreted by failing to account for all the variables (in 2010 a climate scientist claimed that weather stations were picking the heat trails from aircraft in their readings, which, if they were not adjusted for, might produce overestimates of global temperatures – this was reported as having 'skewed' the data). Frequently organisations are accused of having 'skewed' the data deliberately. This usage might lead you to believe that there is something wrong with skewed data, when in fact it is simply a description of the shape of a distribution, and may have been measured entirely accurately. Skew does not imply fraud, as some people think.

Answer the following questions:

1 People sometimes say that the mean of a distribution is the 'best guess' of the value of any random single observation in the distribution. In what sense are they correct?

   (a) If you make a series of many guesses, the total of the errors where you have overestimated the value will balance the total of errors where you underestimated the value.

   (b) The mean will appear more often than any other value.

   (c) Any individual value has a 50/50 chance of being either above or below the mean.

   (d) All of the statements are true.

2 How would you go about discovering which of the two incidents below is more extraordinary?

   (a) A temperature of –6 centigrade in London.

   (b) A temperature of –8 centigrade in Bath.

3 Your firm owns seven different businesses, and the reports of annual profits for each business are as follows:

   3 m   7 m   4 m   6 m   2 m   8 m   19 m

   Which of the following statements is true?

   (a) Half of the reports are between the mean and the mode.

   (b) Half of the reports are in the range.

   (c) Half of the reports are between Q (1) and Q (3).

See page 203 for the answers

Many scores are really a range: IQ tests

Intelligence Quotient, or IQ, tests are popularly thought to measure a person's intelligence. Actually they don't do this. What they do measure is how well a person can perform in an IQ test, which is not the same thing. It has been shown, for instance, that you can learn to do better in an IQ test by practice, and that IQ tests tend to have cultural biases; a highly intelligent warrior from the Amazonian jungle, for instance, may not do well on a standard IQ test simply because his cultural assumptions are different from the people who devised the tests.

Suppose you have a son and a daughter, Sam and Jane; they take an IQ test, and you are told that Sam has scored 98 and Jane has scored 101. A score of 100 is considered 'normal' or 'average'. Do the scores mean that Jane has an above average IQ while Sam has a below average one? Do they mean that Jane is cleverer than Sam? No, because these scores really represent a range, not a single number.

Let's assume they took a well-known variety of the IQ test called the 'Revised Stanford-Binet'. The probable error of this test (not the same as the standard error) is 3%, which means that there is a 1 in 2 probability that any IQ score is correct, plus or minus 3 points. In other words, there is a 1 in 2 chance that Sam's IQ is in the range of 95 to 101, and there is a 1 in 2 chance that Jane's IQ is in the range 98 to 104. Thus it could easily be the case that Sam's IQ is higher than Jane's, that they were both 'above average' or both 'below average'.

Avoid jumping to conclusions: Simpson's paradox

Simpson's paradox is a paradoxical effect that happens when a trend in two separate groups reverses when you combine these groups. It occurs very frequently, so it is important to watch out for when looking for trends in data. Here's a real-life example of how it works:

In the 1970s there was a sex discrimination lawsuit against the University of California at Berkeley, based on the figures for admissions of post graduate students by gender in autumn 1973.

	Applied	Accepted
Male	8442	44%
Female	4321	35%

On the face of it, it looked as if the university was accepting a larger proportion of male applicants than female applicants, and that the difference was too large to be the result of chance.

Each department in the university was examined to find the culprits:

	Male		Female	
Department	Applied	Accepted	Applied	Accepted
A	825	62%	108	82%
B	560	63%	25	68%
C	325	37%	593	34%
D	417	33%	375	35%
E	191	28%	393	24%
F	272	6%	341	7%

When broken down by department, it was found that the situation was reversed: no department was significantly biased against accepting female students, and in fact most departments were slightly biased in favour of female applicants. Further research found that women tended to apply to departments that were harder to get into (because of competition from applicants) and tended to avoid ones that required high mathematics. The researchers suggested, however, that this was because female postgraduate students had been 'shunted' by their socialisation and earlier education towards these departments.[2]

Correlation

Is there a connection between smoking and heart disease? Are people who buy novels likely to own a CD player? Statisticians can examine questions like these to see if two such variables are correlated. No correlation is scored as 0 and a perfect correlation is scored as 1. Negative scores mean that high numbers on one variable are correlated with low scores on the other. Correlations can give clues to a relationship. For example, tall people tend to be heavier – but they do not of themselves prove that one variable is causing changes in the other.

Figure 1.8 shows different kinds of correlation depicted as scattergrams. Correlation is particularly useful in marketing. If your company manufactures yacht fittings and you discover that there is a strong positive

---

[2] Bickel, P. J., Hammel, E. A. and O'Connell, J. W. (1975) 'Sex bias in graduate admissions: Data from Berkeley', *Science*, 7 February, Vol. 187, No. 4175, pp. 398–404.

correlation between a person being a lawyer and a yacht-owner, you could direct a sales effort towards lawyers. Insurance companies are also very interested in correlations.

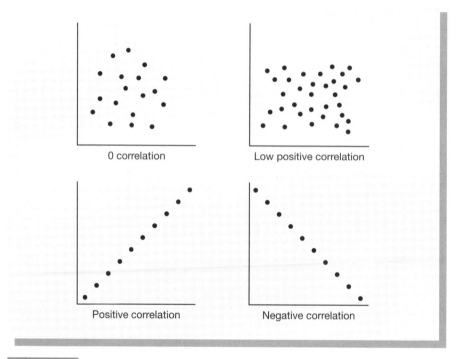

Figure 1.8   Correlation scattergrams

Summary

In this chapter we have looked at the key concepts in handling large amounts of information: different kinds of averages, standard deviation, ranges, skew, the normal distribution, z scores and correlation. In the next chapter we will see how these ideas are extended to analyse these data and how to make estimates from samples, as in surveys.

2

Analysing large amounts of information: market surveys, polls and social behaviour

How do we know, say, that 50% of British men in their thirties use cologne, or that Generation Y only reads books for nine minutes a day? Did someone ask every single person in the group and then add up all their answers? Of course not! They used statistical techniques on much smaller samples of the group to arrive at an estimate. And if they used these techniques properly, their results should be reasonably accurate.

The trouble is that many surveys and polls don't use proper statistical methods. And even when they do, the results are often misunderstood or misrepresented by others. Frequently, it is not that the calculations are incorrect, but that the wrong things have been tested, or the wrong questions have been asked, or that the conclusions drawn go far beyond the evidence. Now that PowerPoint is so widely used, many people feel confident in making slick-looking visual presentations of statistical findings that they themselves have not understood; in many circumstances, it has become normal to assume that all the figures quoted to you by the 'other side' are unreliable until proved otherwise.

This chapter introduces statistical methods, and then discusses basic steps you can take to check if other people have done their studies properly. In the second half of the chapter, some more advanced statistical tests are introduced; if you find this kind of thing tiresome, it is OK to miss this part of the chapter.

Analysing data

Statistics is the science of analysing data. It tells us how data can be collected, organised and analysed, and how to draw conclusions from the data correctly. Without statistics, it would be impossible to perform the calculations behind many familiar things such as:

- political polls;
- the popularity of a website;
- monthly unemployment figures;
- the top 20 music albums;
- the quality control of consumer products;
- the audience ratings for TV programmes;
- the planning of marketing campaigns.

Statistics are used intensively in business and there are a large number of statistical tests available. In this section we will look at the concept of sampling, review some of the commonly used statistical tests, and then see how to interpret the results through statistical inference.

It takes skill and judgement to choose the appropriate test for the circumstances. Suffice it to say that statisticians are not made overnight, and that the purpose of presenting the tests here is to give you a 'feel' for the kinds of manipulations that statisticians can perform on raw data; getting a complete grasp of the subject will require further study, preferably under the guidance of a teacher. You will find that tests often require the use of special tables – these are not included in this book, but you will be able to find them in many specialist textbooks.

Sampling

Suppose you want to conduct a survey of German consumers. Clearly, it would be a huge undertaking to interview every single person in the population, so you decide to survey a smaller number of people in the hope that you can generalise about the whole population from the results you get; this is called sampling. But what if you only interviewed people living in Stuttgart? Your results probably wouldn't be very representative of everyone living in Germany.

Important: to get a representative sample, everyone in the population should have the same chance of being chosen for the sample.

Suppose that you make batteries that are guaranteed to last for a certain amount of time, and you want to test the batteries rolling off the production line to see if they are up to standard. If you tested every battery to the end of its life, you wouldn't have any to sell, so you have to take a sample. But if you only took the last 500 batteries made on Friday afternoons as your sample, it would not be representative, since not every battery would have an equal chance of being tested.

Terminology: population

In statistics, 'population' doesn't only refer to people; it is used to mean any group of things you want to generalise about. When you test some of your batteries, you are sampling the 'population' of the batteries you make.

Census or sample?

If you make a complete study of a population, you are taking a 'census'. Ideally, you would always take a census, because this gives you the most accurate count, but there are several kinds of situations in which it is necessary to take a sample rather than a census:

1 A census may simply cost too much. If you are conducting market research into the preferences of Japanese consumers, for instance, it would be too expensive to interview every individual Japanese consumer, so you must take a sample of them.

2 Lack of time. Political polls, for example, often have to be conducted very quickly.

3 Bias. A vast census project can easily produce more errors than a sample which has been obtained carefully, due to the great difficulty of managing the census. Such errors will produce biased results.

4 Testing a product to destruction is a part of quality control. As mentioned earlier, if you did this with every item, you would have none left to sell.

5 A new drug is for future generations as well as the present one. Since it is impossible to test people who haven't yet been born, a sample of the present population is taken to represent future generations too.

Induction and deduction

Using the characteristics of the sample to generalise about its parent population is called 'induction'. If 3% of your sample of batteries are below standard and you have sampled a representative selection of batteries, you can assume by induction that approximately 3% of all the batteries you make are below standard.

'Deduction' works the other way around; if you know that 3% of all the batteries are below standard, you can deduce that, on average, any carton of batteries being sent out has 3% of substandard batteries.

Making sure the sample is representative

This can be harder than it seems. You have to be very careful to define the population as well as the sample. Sampling consumers in central Stuttgart tells you about consumers in central Stuttgart, not about consumers in the south of Germany, which is a different, larger population which includes consumers in central Stuttgart. You might well get results from your survey which turn out to be relevant to a wider population, but you wouldn't know for certain until you sampled the wider population. This may seem obvious, but in practice it is very easy to jump to false conclusions.

Suppose, for example, you are an MP who gets lots of letters from your constituents complaining about a steep rise in crime in your constituency. Are you entitled to say that most of your constituents are worried about a rise in crime, based on the letters you have received? Certainly not; the letters are not a representative sample of all your constituents, many of whom would never dream of writing you a letter. The letters are a 'biased' sample; we would need to investigate further if we wanted to discover what kinds of people wrote the letters – for instance, a religious group or an activist organisation with a specific agenda might have told all its members to write to you complaining about crime.

One way to get a representative sample is to give every item in a population a number and then pick numbers at random for your sample. You can get random numbers from most personal computer (PC) spreadsheets, or from published random number tables. This method would work if you were sampling an electoral roll or a list of customers.

Example

You decide to conduct a consumer survey by sampling an electoral list. You number every voter and you open your random number tables and start reading off numbers from the beginning. You are introducing a bias! If you always start at the beginning of a random number table, or if your spreadsheet always generates the same random sequence, this may affect your samples. Opening the tables, stabbing your finger on a number and starting from there would be better; strictly speaking, it is 'pseudo-random', but it is good enough for most purposes. Making up random numbers is not; it has been shown statistically that people have strong unconscious preferences for certain numbers, so don't cheat!

Real-life stories   **Opinion polls in real life**

A famous example of an unsuccessful opinion poll was conducted in the US in 1936 by a magazine called the *Literary Digest* to predict the results of an election. A sample of 10 million subscribers to the magazine, who also had telephones, was drawn from a list that had been used to predict the 1932 election successfully. In 1936, the results of the sample caused the magazine to predict that Landon (a Republican) would beat Roosevelt (a Democrat) for the presidency by a very wide margin, but in the real election, Roosevelt won. Bias in the sample was due to the fact that people who had telephones and subscribed to magazines in 1936 were better off, and tended to be Republicans.

The moral of all this is simply that very many samples are biased, not because of deliberate chicanery, but because of the difficulty of obtaining a truly random sample. Inferences drawn from samples which may not be random should therefore be treated with caution.

Test yourself: Part 4

1 In statistics, a sample is:

(a) A number produced by raw data analysis.

(b) A representative subset of a population.

(c) A set of things, measurements or people that have something in common.

2 There are an estimated 5 million 'early adopters' of new computer technology in your country, who will buy any new technology as soon as it comes out. You conduct a telephone survey of 100 subscribers to your computer magazine to ask them their opinions of New Technology X. There are 35,000 subscribers to the magazine, and you telephone the first hundred people whose surnames begin with C. 70% of the people you call are positive about New Technology X. You publish a survey that claims that 70% early adopters in your country are positive about New Technology X.

Based on what you have read so far in this chapter, explain why your survey does not provide evidence in support of the results you claim.

▶

▶

3 In a warehouse of canned foods, you assign a number to all the cans with red labels and select a few of these at random using a table of random numbers. Of what population have you taken a sample?

See page 203 for the answers.

Statistical inference

The main reason why you take a sample of a population is that you want to make inferences about the population after examining the sample, such as estimating the mean of the population and its standard deviation. There are two kinds of statistical inference, *estimation* and *hypothesis testing*.

Estimation is when you take a random sample from a population and use it to estimate some parameter of the population. A typical estimate might read: 'On the basis of a random sample of 600 consumers it is estimated that the percentage of the population of consumers who prefer the new soap powder is 72%, with a 95% confidence interval from 58% to 79%'. The last phrase means that the probability that the interval does not contain the true percentage of the population is 5%.

If you take a sample of a population and test it to see if a theory you have about the population is true or not, you are testing your 'hypothesis'. We will look at hypothesis testing later on.

Estimation

As mentioned above, if you have taken a sample properly, it will share a lot of characteristics, such as its distribution, dispersion and typical values, with the larger population from which it has been taken. For instance, the best estimate of the mean of a population is the mean of the sample (although, as we will see below, it is unlikely to be exactly the same). Let's look at how to estimate the standard deviation from a sample:

Example

This is calculated slightly differently from the method shown on page 15.

Step 1. Take the sample set (6, 9, 11, 15), and work out the mean:

$$(6 + 9 + 11 + 15) = 41 \div 4 = 10.25.$$

Step 2. Calculate the deviations from the mean:

$$6 - 10.25 = -4.25$$
$$9 - 10.25 = -1.25$$
$$11 - 10.25 = 0.75$$
$$15 - 10.25 = 4.75$$

Step 3. Square the deviations:

$$-4.25^2 = 18.06$$
$$-1.25^2 = 1.56$$
$$0.75^2 = 0.56$$
$$475^2 = 22.56$$

Step 4. Add the squares:

$$18.06 + 1.56 + 0.56 + 22.56 = 42.74$$

Step 5. This is the step that is different from the method on page 15. Divide by the number of observations minus 1.

$$42.74 \div (4 - 1) = 14.25$$

This is your estimate of the 'variance'.

Step 6. Find the square root:

$$\sqrt{14.25} = 3.8.$$

This is your estimate of the standard deviation.

The reason why you subtract 1 from the number of observations is that if you use the earlier method when estimating the population's standard deviation from a sample, your estimate will always be slightly small because the mean of the sample is likely to be different from the true mean of the distribution. Suppose that on average your sample readings are slightly big compared with average members of the whole population. Your sample mean will then be somewhat larger than the true mean, and when you calculate the deviations from the sample mean you get smaller values than if you had calculated the deviations from the true mean (which you do not know). You compensate for this effect by dividing by $n - 1$ instead of n to estimate the standard deviation of the population. n is just shorthand for the number of observations.

Sampling error, standard error and the central limit theorem

Suppose you take two samples of the same population and get slightly different results. You take a third sample and get even more different results. Does this mean you have made a mistake? Probably not; supposing the standard deviation of your first sample was 10 and the mean was 80, and the mean of the second sample was 72, you could say that, working from your first sample, 68% of all scores would be between 70 and 90, so your second sample's mean of 72 is not surprising. The point is that you don't expect to get identical results from several samples – there will be some variation. This variation is called the 'sampling error'. But what if your third sample's mean was 40? Since 95% of the population should be between 60 and 100, this sample is either a mistake, or it is in the 5% outside two standard deviations from the mean; it is out on the tail of the normal curve.

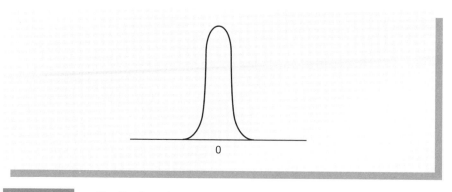

0

Figure 2.1   Distribution of means

If you took many samples and drew a graph of their means, it might look like the curve in Figure 2.1. The distribution of the means will be much closer together than the distribution of the scores within the samples; in other words, the standard deviation of the means of the samples is much smaller than the standard deviation of all the scores in the samples. The standard deviation of the means is called the 'standard error'. If you know, or have estimated, the true standard deviation of the population, you expect the standard error for samples of size n to be:

Standard error = Standard deviation ÷ √(Size of sample)

In other words, if the standard deviation of the population is 10 and you take a series of samples of size 100 and calculate their means, you expect the standard error of these means to be 10 ÷ √100 = 1.

Another feature of the standard deviation of the means is that a theorem known as the 'central limit theorem' tells us that as you take bigger and bigger samples from a population, the distribution of the means of the samples will tend towards a normal distribution, even if the population itself isn't normal. This is one of the reasons why we can still make calculations using the normal distribution even if we aren't sure of the shape of the parent population. Although the curve in Figure 2.1 doesn't look normal, if it were redrawn on an appropriate scale it would be immediately apparent that it was close to a normal curve.

Confidence

So now that we know that our samples will have some error, how can we quantify the error? We know that if our sample was 100% of the total population, we could be 100% confident of the accuracy of our calculations. In many cases, we would be happy with being 99% confident, or 90%, or perhaps only 60%.

Fortunately, quite small samples can give us a high confidence level. You can have 95% confidence that:

Population mean – Sample mean ≤
([1.96 × Sample standard deviation] ÷ √Sample size)

where the population mean – sample mean is the positive value of the difference between the two means.

Alternatively, you could say that you have 95% confidence that the population mean is in the interval:

[Sample mean – {(1.96 × Standard deviation) ÷ √n},
Sample mean + {(1 .96 × Standard deviation) ÷ √n}]

Example

If you take a random sample of 64 potential customers to see how much they spend annually on holidays and you find that the average spent is £2,000 with a standard deviation of 500, you can say that you are 95% confident that the mean of the money spent on holidays by the total population is 2,000 ± (500 ÷ √64).

2,000 ± (500 + √64) = 2,000 ± (500 ÷ 8) = 2,000 ± 62.50

In other words, although this is only a small sample, you are 95% sure that the average sum spent by the population on holidays is between 1,937.50 and 2,062.50. This range is called a 'confidence interval'.

The confidence intervals that are most frequently used are 99%, 95% and 90%. We have just seen how to find the confidence interval for 95%; you can have 90% confidence that:

Population mean – Sample mean ≤
[(1.6449 × Sample standard deviation) ÷ √Sample size]

and you can have 99% confidence that:

Population mean – Sample mean ≤
[(2.5758 × Sample standard deviation) ÷ √Sample size]

Significance levels

You may hear statisticians talk about levels of 'significance' rather than 'confidence'. The significance level is the probability of making an error of commission, or saying something is so when it is not; a 95% confidence level is the same as using a 5% significance level, or a 5% chance of being wrong. There is a convention that a 5% significance level is called 'significant' and that a 1% significance level is called 'highly significant'.

Finding the sample size for a confidence level

You may wonder why a confidence level of 99% or even 99.9% isn't always used. The reason is that to obtain higher degrees of confidence you need to allow a wider range of possibilities. For example, if you found that the percentage of customers who were willing to buy a new product was between 6% and 90% with a 99.9% confidence level, it wouldn't be very helpful, so you would reduce the confidence level to produce a more meaningful finding.

Suppose you wanted to know how big a sample to take to find the mean annual income of households in a certain area with 90% confidence. Assume that you know that the income is normally distributed, that the standard deviation is £2,000 and you want the confidence interval to be £1,600 wide.

The upper and lower limits of the confidence interval will be:

Lower limit = Sample mean –
{(1.6449 × Sample standard deviation) ÷ √Sample size},
Upper limit = Sample mean +
{(1.6449 × Sample standard deviation) ÷ √Sample size}

The width of the interval is the upper limit minus the lower limit which equals (2 × 1.6449 × Sample standard deviation ÷ √Sample size). You want this to be 1,600, so we solve:

$$1,600 = [2 \times 1.6449 \times 2,000] \div \sqrt{n}$$

This gives

$$1,600 \times \sqrt{n} = [2 \times 1.6449 \times 2,000] \div 1,600$$
$$\sqrt{n} = [2 \times 1.6449 \times 2,000] \div 1,600$$
$$\sqrt{n} = 4.112$$

So the Sample size n = 4.112 × 4.112 = 16.9. You can't take a sample of 16.9 households so you round this up to the nearest whole number, 17.

Test yourself: Part 5

1 In year 1, the average sales achieved by each salesperson is £81,000 with a standard deviation of 9. In year 2, the average sales achieved was £78,000 with a standard deviation of 12. If salesperson X achieved £93,000 in each year, in which year did she perform better in relation to the rest of the team?

2 An anthropologist takes a random sample of the length of the blowpipes used by an Amazonian tribe. From a sample of 9 blowpipes, the mean length is 70 inches. The anthropologist knows from earlier studies that the standard deviation is 3 inches. Rounding to the nearest inch, a 95% confidence interval for the mean length is:

(a) 68 to 70 inches.

(b) 69 to 71 inches.

(c) 67 to 73 inches.

See page 203 for the answers.

Spotting poor conclusions in survey results

In many situations it is extremely difficult to get a representative sample of a population. This does not prevent spurious claims from being made about populations. Often, the people making such claims simply don't know how to check that a sample is representative and are not aware of the dangers of bias.

Anatomy of a survey

A well-known women's magazine published the results of a two-page survey on the eating habits of its readers. In the first paragraph it states that over 10,000 individuals responded to a questionnaire, but doesn't say how many were sent out. The second paragraph opens with a statement that 67% of respondents are bored with food scares; this is the last time that it is pointed out that the percentages quoted are of people who responded to the questionnaire. Fair enough, you might think, but what about the statement in the fourth paragraph, '1 in 5 readers snatches meals on the move once or twice a week'? Respondents have now become readers, implying that the respondents to the questionnaire are a representative sample of the total population of readers. This seems unlikely; perhaps the people who didn't respond to the questionnaire were too busy to do so, and perhaps their eating habits were different from the respondents'. For instance, non-responders may 'snatch meals on the move' more often because they are so busy.

The statements get broader and broader; in the final paragraph we are told that 'it is clear that Britain is now a nation of wine lovers because '89% of you drink at home'. The respondents are now taken to represent the population of Britain. Since the article has already implied that all the respondents were women, for this reason alone they cannot possibly be a representative sample of the British population.

There are two highlighted boxes featured. One opens with the statement that 'people in Wales and the South-West are the least likely to believe that food can be sexy', while the other one informs us that more than half of readers buy frozen pastry. Once again, the sample is certainly not representative of the population of Wales and the South-West, and is unlikely to be representative of the population of readers of the magazine.

Is it unfair to be too critical of all this? The writers of this kind of article have a genuine difficulty; they must make the article interesting and readable, and so they cannot tabulate the data and report it in the dry way that, say, a statistical office does. However, readers of the article are being given the impression that the sample is representative of the populations referred to; this is plainly untrue.

Suppose you sent out a survey to all the readers of the magazine which asked 'Do you like answering surveys?' and 90% of the respondents said that they did. Would you be entitled to state that 90% of the readers of the magazine liked answering surveys? That would be a ridiculous conclusion, because it is highly unlikely that the respondents would be a representative sample – people who don't like answering surveys would be unlikely to complete the survey.

This kind of distortion frequently appears in advertisements: '8 out of 10 dentists who expressed a preference preferred Brand X'. We are not told how many dentists were asked, how many of those who were asked did not 'express a preference' or whether those who were asked were a representative sample of all the dentists in the country, although this is implied. Since professionals such as dentists are generally unhappy about endorsing products, it seems likely that the majority would politely 'not express a preference'.

Problems of validity: two real-life cases

Video nasties

Back in the 1980s, with the advent of videoplayers there was a boom in the sales of lurid low-budget horror films that came to be known as 'video nasties'. This engendered a nationwide hysteria that young children were being exposed to obscene and depraved videos that would mark them for life. Arrests were made, videos were seized, and a bill was brought to Parliament to regulate the circulation of videos. In support of the bill, research was produced that purported to show that 40% of six-year-olds had seen video nasties. This information turned out to be the result of questionnaires given to 6,000 six-year-olds, of which 47 had responded. The questionnaire listed a number of famous video nasties and asked respondents if they had seen any of them; 17 out of the 47 said that they had, giving the 40% figure.

Once again, we can immediately recognise our old friend, the non-representative sample. But perhaps that could be forgiven – the research was ongoing, and these were interim results produced in a hurry at a time when the issue was a major political issue in the UK. What was much more problematic was the method used to try to discover whether children had seen the video nasties. Asking a small child 'Have you seen X?' might, after all, elicit a positive, but false, response.

Two other academics conducted similar research, this time asking 11-year-olds if they had seen any of a list of completely fictitious video nasty titles, and obtained 68% positive responses, demonstrating that the original research had probably been invalid – it had tested what children claimed to have seen, not what they had actually seen.

The terrible case of dihydrogen monoxide

This hoax is so much fun that it has been perpetrated many times since it was first invented in the late 1980s. Politicians, local newspapers, city councils and other public bodies have all fallen for it at various times. One 14-year-old schoolboy, Nathan Zohner, managed to win a science prize by conducting the hoax in the form of a survey. He presented 50 schoolmates with a petition to control or ban a chemical, 'dihydrogen monoxide', on the grounds that, among other things, it causes sweating, in its gaseous state it can cause severe burns, and that it has been found in cancerous tumors. This odourless, colourless substance, said the petition, is used in the manufacture of chemical and biological weapons, and is consumed by elite athletes to improve their performance, but thousands of people die every year from accidentally inhaling dihydrogen monoxide.

▶

> Nathan found that 47 of the 50 people he asked were willing to sign the petition. Only one person realised what dihydrogen monoxide really was: water (H_2O). His conclusion? That people are gullible and the respondents didn't read the petition critically.
>
> The point here is that it is relatively easy to dress up something in such a way that you can persuade people to support your (spurious) conclusions. This seems to be a particular problem in areas such as alternative medicine, in which certain types of customer are especially vulnerable to deceit.

Bias in samples

The examples of non-representative samples in the previous section are fairly obvious once you are alert to them, but bias can creep into samples in more subtle ways. The problem is that only truly random samples work perfectly in statistics, and in many situations it is too expensive, if not impossible, to take a truly random sample. When presented with a sample, ask yourself the question, 'Did everything in the population have an equal chance of being in the sample?' If not, the sample is not random and therefore has bias.

Opinion pollsters and market researchers don't usually use random samples; instead, they use 'stratified' samples or 'cluster' samples.

Stratified samples and cluster samples

Cluster sampling is taking a random sample of 'clusters' of members of the population. If you wanted to survey a sample of the households in a big city, you could pick a sample of small areas (clusters) – say, individual streets – and interview every household in the sample clusters. This is a cheap way of obtaining a sample, but it will be biased, since it is not completely random.

Stratified samples are obtained by separating the population into different sets or 'strata' and then taking random samples from each stratum. Typical criteria for separating the population into strata might be:

▦ Male or female?
▦ Age: under 20
         20 – 30
         31 – 40
         41 – 50
         51 – 60

■ Occupation:
>   Professional
>   Clerical
>   Blue collar
>   Other.

For the stratification to work, the strata must be mutually exclusive. A member of the population should fall into only one of the strata.

Suppose a team of market researchers are told to go out into the street and each interview 30 people under 50 and 30 people over 50. To make their work easier, they may tend to avoid people who look about 50 years old, thus introducing a bias into the sample, which will contain fewer people in their late forties or early fifties than it should.

Another problem with this kind of interview is that the researchers may avoid difficult-looking people, which will also introduce a bias into the sample. Experts on market research and polls wage an unceasing war against bias, but the war is never won.

Real-life stories **Trying to measure ethnicity in the UK – category problems**

With the praiseworthy aim of eliminating racial prejudice, many organisations in the UK ask people filling in forms to answer the following:

I would describe myself as:

>   White
>>   White British
>>   White Irish
>>   Other White
>   Mixed
>   Asian or Asian British
>>   Indian
>>   Pakistani
>>   Bangladeshi
>>   Other Asian
>   Black or Black British
>>   Black Caribbean

▶

Black African

Other Black

Chinese or Other

Chinese

Any other ethnic group

Ethnicity is an extremely problematic concept and most scholars now reject the idea, prevalent in the nineteenth and early twentieth centuries, that 'peoples' or 'tribes' are, in general, racially, linguistically and culturally homogeneous groups with a common descent. For example, recent historical study of the Dark Ages has shown that the barbarian hordes who invaded the Roman empire were much more ethnically diverse than had previously been realised. The barbarian leaders Edica and his son Odoacer, for instance, were described at different times by various contemporaries as 'Huns', 'Thuringians', 'Eruls', 'Rugians' and 'Goths'. It is now clear that these terms should not be taken as descriptions of homogeneous ethnic groups at all, as used to be thought, but are more likely to have been names used to describe political federations of linguistically and culturally diverse warbands. In the past, as today, people mixed with one another, and their conceptions of ethnic identity often changed.

These days, most academics agree that ethnicity is best seen as a highly subjective phenomenon, and that the best that can be said about it is that if you say you are ethnically X, then we should accept that you think you are ethnically X – which is quite different from attempting to measure your ethnicity by some 'objective' criteria.

This state of affairs is not very satisfactory for governments, who are interested in how to classify and control the various populations within their states, and don't seem to have quite caught up with the subtleties of academe. In a Green Paper of July 2007 Prime Minister Gordon Brown declared that there was a need for a 'national identity that we can all hold in common: the overarching factor – British citizenship – that brings the nation together'.[1] This illustrates that, from the point of view of the state, the issue of national identity is essentially a question of loyalty. This issue is often portrayed as a very new, very modern problem, but in fact, as many historians have demonstrated, it is thousands of years old: governments have always engaged in forms of nation-building.

The Office of National Statistics (ONS) shed some interesting light on this problem in a 2006 publication.[2] In it, it is recognised that ethnicity is subjective, and that therefore what should be measured in censuses and surveys is how people 'self-identify' – in other words, what they themselves say they are. From the statistician's point of view, this still presents problems, because in order to conduct the analysis we need some categories of data. If we just invite people to invent their own categories, as is sometimes done, then we cannot be sure that there are no potential overlaps between categories. For example, if I say I am 'Irish' and you say

---

[1]   *The Governance of Britain*, presented to Parliament by the Secretary of State for Justice and Lord Chancellor, HMSO, July 2007, p. 53.

[2]   Dobbs, J., Green, H. and Zealey, L. (2006) *Focus on Ethnicity and Religion*, Office of National Statistics, Crown copyright.

you are 'White', would that necessarily exclude me from the definition of 'White'? For this reason, the ONS has generally asked people to use pre-defined categories since it first introduced questions about ethnicity in the mid-1970s, although in the 2011 census there does appear to have been a question inviting respondents to invent their own categories.

Before the mid-1970s, various other approaches were used to identify ethnicity, such as asking where people were born, where their parents were born, and the languages they spoke, but these clearly fail to capture, say, third generation immigrants, and didn't necessarily distinguish between people who would self-identify as, say, Irish, English, Welsh or Scottish. Since the 1970s, the ONS has altered the categories of ethnicity used in its surveys more than once in its efforts to make them more meaningful. The aim has not been to capture all the ethnic groups in England and Wales, mainly because many of them are so small that in survey (not census) data, analysis would be unreliable because of sampling problems. Even though there are now 16 ethnic categories recommended for use by the ONS, they still remain quite a blunt instrument, and are designed to analyse trends among a few 'majority minorities', rather than among the many small ones.

Statisticians tend to be a high-minded bunch, and are careful to explain the limitations of their analyses to anyone who will listen. But it's easy to see how people in very small ethnic groups might potentially suffer injustice at the hands of bureaucrats who want to lump them in with some larger pre-ordained category.

We have now covered the main concepts in sampling for surveys. In the next section, we will look at a variety of statistical tests that are in common use. It is not necessary to master these in order to move on to the following chapters, so you can skip this section if you wish, and refer to it later if, for instance, you encounter a discussion of statistical tests in a research report.

Choosing the right statistical test

There are many statistical tests, each of which can only be applied in certain circumstances; it is often quite difficult to decide which tests to use. Fortunately, there are flow charts to help choose the test you need. Since we only cover a few of the tests at a basic level in this book, a flow chart is not provided here; if you decide to get deeper into testing, you will find flow charts in the majority of heavyweight statistics textbooks.

The first step is to decide which of the following five categories your objective comes under:

1 analysing the relationship of two or more variables;
2 analysing the relationship between two variables;

3 comparing two or more populations;

4 comparing two populations;

5 describing one population.

Each of these categories branches off into subcategories, so you gradually work your way through the flow chart until you find the appropriate test to use.

Parametric and non-parametric tests

'Parametric' refers to the fact that a test makes assumptions about the parameters of a distribution, such as the mean and standard deviation. The principal uses of parametric tests are for testing your own assumptions about a population and for comparing samples to see if they came from the same or different populations. In this chapter, we assume a normal distribution, although the tests may be 'robust', which means that they often work for other distributions too. The t-test, described below, is an example of a parametric test. Tests which make no assumptions about distributions are called non-parametric and several examples are described below.

Degrees of freedom

A concept which is used in many of the tests is that of the 'degrees of freedom' of a sample. On page 33 we saw that when calculating the standard deviation for a sample, we divide by $n - 1$, the number of observations minus 1; $n - 1$ is called the degrees of freedom (df). For example, a sample with 25 observations has 24 degrees of freedom.

Type 1 and Type 2 errors

Suppose you are playing Russian roulette; it is your turn to put the gun to your head. Your alternative hypothesis is that there is no bullet in the gun's chamber and your null hypothesis is that there is a bullet in the chamber. If you pull the trigger and shoot yourself, you have committed a Type 1 error. If you refuse to pull the trigger and it turns out that there was no bullet in the chamber, you have committed a Type 2 error by wrongly rejecting your alternative hypothesis. But that is fine, because you would much prefer to commit many Type 2 errors than to commit one Type 1 error – you want to stay alive!

To calculate the probability of making a Type 2 error, you have to work out the probability of rejecting the null hypothesis when it is false. This is called finding the 'power' of a test. The probability of making a Type 2 error is written as β, so the power is 1– β. Finding a power can be difficult; you must know the sampling distribution of the test statistic when the alternative hypothesis is true, and you must also know the values of the test statistic which cause you to reject the null hypothesis.

The t-test

We saw on page 34 that different samples from the same population usually have different means and that the standard deviation of the means of samples is smaller than the standard deviation of all the observations in the sample. T scores are used in a similar way to Z scores for small samples. If you think that your population is normal but you don't know its standard deviation and you can only take a small sample, you can use the t-test to avoid the errors you would otherwise make in estimating from a small sample.

If we let the t difference in means = standard error of difference in means, we find that the distribution of t is not usually normal, although it tends towards the normal as the size of the sample increases (see the central limit theorem on page 34).

Example

Suppose you have received a number of complaints about the time it takes for your company to deliver its products to its customers. You decide to check the delivery times for a random sample of 20 items. Adding the sample delivery times together gives you 234, and adding the squares of each sample delivery time gives you 3,048. You work out that the mean delivery time of the samples is $234 \div 20 = 11.7$, and that the standard deviation of the sample with 19 degrees of freedom is:

$$\sqrt{\{[3{,}048 - (2342 \div 20)] \div 19\}}$$
$$= \sqrt{[(3{,}048 - 2{,}737.8) \div 19]}$$
$$= \sqrt{(310.20 \div 19)}$$
$$= 4.041$$

You now look up the value of t in t tables and get 2.0930, so you can work out that the confidence interval is:

$$\text{Mean} \pm [\text{t} \times (\text{Standard deviation} \div \sqrt{\text{Number of sample}}]$$
$$11.7 \pm [2.0930 \times (4.041 + \sqrt{20})] =$$
$$11.7 \pm (2.0930 \times 0.90362) =$$
$$11.7 \pm 1.9$$

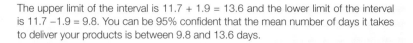

The upper limit of the interval is 11.7 + 1.9 = 13.6 and the lower limit of the interval is 11.7 −1.9 = 9.8. You can be 95% confident that the mean number of days it takes to deliver your products is between 9.8 and 13.6 days.

F-test

The F-test, or variance ratio test, works with very small samples. It compares the spread of scores of two samples from normal distributions; like the t-test it is robust, and works well unless the distribution is a very long way from the normal. If the ratio of the sample variances is larger than the value of F given in tables for F, then there is a significant difference between the two variances.

Example

Suppose you are considering marketing a computer product for use in cars. It would work best if it was situated by the gear stick, on the left of the driver, and naturally you are concerned to know if potential users will be willing to operate the keyboard with their left hand, given that most people are right-handed. One of the tests you could conduct would be to see if people made more errors on the keyboard with their left hands than with their right; the F-test will tell you if the variance of left-handed scores is significantly different from that of the right-handed scores. Say the sample of left-handed scores is $n_1 = 8$ and the sample of right-handed scores is $n_2 = 12$.

Step 1. Calculate the variance of each set of scores by the standard deviation method for samples. Say the results are 8.3 for the left-handed test and 2.2 for the right-handed one.

Step 2. Calculate the ratio. 8.3 ÷ 2.2 = 3.07.

Step 3. The F tables give you critical values for this ratio for samples of different sizes and at different significance levels. In some books there is a different F table for each of the commonly desired significance levels and in others they are combined into one table. Work out the degrees of freedom for the larger of the two variances, which is 8.3. $n_1 = 8$, so there are 7 degrees of freedom. Do the same for the smaller variance 2.2. $n_2 = 12$, so there are 11 degrees of freedom.

Step 4. Table 2.1 shows an extract from a table for F with 5% significance. Looking down the column for 7 df for n_1, we see that the df for n_2, which is 11, falls between the rows df 10 and df 12. The critical F values given are 3.95 and 3.61, both of which are higher than our ratio, 3.07, so we must conclude with 95% confidence that the variance of the left-handed scores is significantly different from the variance of the right-handed scores.

Table 2.1 F table extract: 5% significance

Degrees of freedom for n_2	Degrees of freedom for n_1		
	7	8	9
9	4.20	4.10	4.03
10	3.95	3.85	3.78
12	3.61	3.51	3.44

The chi-squared test

'Chi' is the Greek letter χ, which is used as a symbol in statistics. 'Chi-squared' just means χ^2. The chi-squared test is used to test if there is an association between independent conditions, for example, if you want to see if there is an association between being a smoker and getting lung cancer, or between being a trainee doctor and being suicidal. It can also be used to test the goodness of fit between a theory and the observations. For example, you could apply the test to check out a theory that people tend to prefer certain numbers when asked to think of any number.

Suppose you manage a number of retail outlets, and you know from experience that 25% of your customers pay cash, 25% pay by cheque, 25% pay by credit card and 25% pay using the company's own charge card. You take a sample of 400 sales receipts from a particular week and find the following results:

Cash	Cheque	Credit card	Charge card	Total
120	110	80	90	400

Suppose that what you expected to see was:

Cash	Cheque	Credit card	Charge card	Total
100	100	100	100	400

These are your 'expected values'. Do your actual results fit your theory based on your past experience? The chi-squared goodness of fit test uses the term:

$\chi2$ = [The sum of (observation squared ÷ Expected value)]
  – Number of observations
  = $(120^2 ÷ 100) + (110^2 ÷ 100) + (80^2 ÷ 100) + (90^2 ÷ 100) - 400$
  = $144 + 121 + 64 + 81 - 400 = 10$

You must now look up the critical value of χ^2 for the degrees of freedom and desired degree of confidence. If the value you have obtained from your data is less than this critical value, you can conclude with your desired degree of confidence that your data is incompatible with your theory, but if your value is greater than the critical one, you should conclude the opposite.

Suppose we want to be 95% confident of our conclusions; this is a 5% level of significance. Table 2.2 shows an extract from chi-squared tables.

Table 2.2 Extract from chi-squared table: 5% significance

Degrees of freedom	Chi-squared
1	3.481
2	5.991
3	7.815
4	9.488
5	11.071

We have 3 degrees of freedom in our example, so the critical value for chi-squared is 7.815. Our result is 10, so we must conclude with 95% confidence that the observations do not fit our theory, and it is necessary to conduct further statistical tests to find out why this is so. The chi-squared test is a 'non-parametric' test, because it makes no assumptions about distributions or other parameters. We will now look at some other non-parametric tests.

Other non parametric tests

Non-parametric tests are very useful for dealing with ranked data. If you conduct a market survey into customer satisfaction, and ask people to rate their opinions as Excellent, Good, Fair and Poor, the information you collected would be 'ranked'. You could give a value to each category, say Excellent = 4, Good 3, Fair = 2 and Poor = 1, but the difference between these values does not mean anything, so you couldn't work out means or variances for these data.

Here are two non-parametric tests that you may come across when dealing with data that is ranked or not normal in some way.

The Wilcoxon rank sum test

The Wilcoxon test compares two populations when the data is ranked or not normal. It tells you if the locations of the populations are different. For instance, you could use it to test the effectiveness of a painkiller compared with aspirin, if the people you tested rated its effectiveness on a scale.

The Kruskal-Wallis test

This test compares two or more populations when the data is not normal.

Hypothesis testing

If you take a sample of a population and test it to see if a theory you have about the population is true or not, you are testing your 'hypothesis'. For example, when we looked at the F-test, we were testing a hypothesis that the z variances were different. In this section we will explore some of the terminology of the theory of hypothesis testing.

Suppose your company is considering the introduction of a new soap powder, Wonder Soap, and you want to know whether consumers will prefer it to a competitor's product, Super Soap. You decide to ask 200 consumers to wash two loads of clothes, one with Wonder Soap and the other with Super Soap, and then to tell you which result they prefer. When the trials are over, you hope to be able to make the decision about whether or not to put Wonder Soap on the market. If almost all the consumers prefer Wonder Soap, then you feel confident that it should be marketed, but if they cannot tell the difference, then you think the plan should be reconsidered.

The alternative hypothesis

One way of describing the aim of your trials is to say that you are testing the 'alternative hypothesis' that people will prefer Wonder Soap to Super Soap. This can be written as:

$$H1:p>0.5$$

where H1 is the alternative hypothesis and p is the proportion of the population that prefers Wonder Soap, p>0.5 means that more than half the people will prefer Wonder Soap.

The null hypothesis

The null hypothesis is the statement that you hope is not true; in the case of the soap powder, the null hypothesis (H0) is that people do not prefer Wonder Soap to Super Soap. Tests are often designed to see if there has been a change in a population, so the null hypothesis is often, 'There is no change in the population', which is why it is called 'null', meaning 'nothing', or no change. Statistical tests are always performed to test the truth of the null hypothesis first.

The test statistic

We've already seen that the alternative hypothesis for the Wonder Soap trials is Hl:p>0.5. The null hypothesis can be written as:

$$H0:p = 0.5.$$

This means that if half of the people in the trials prefer Wonder Soap, the null hypothesis holds true.

You test the truth of the null hypothesis by means of a 'test statistic', written as T. T is a statistic that will tend to have certain values when H0 is true and different values when H1 is true. In the case of our example, T is just the number of times that Wonder Soap is preferred in the trials. When the null hypothesis is true, the distribution of T is called the null distribution of the test statistic.

Type 1 and Type 2 errors

A Type 1 error is made if the null hypothesis is rejected when it is true. Significance levels (see page 36) describe the probability of making a Type 1 error; if the significance level is 0.05, it means that the chance of making a Type 1 error is 5%.

The binomial theorem

Like the normal distribution, the binomial distribution is useful for calculating probability. To understand how it works we must consider the 'Bernoulli trial', which refers to any experiment with only two possible outcomes.

Bernoulli trials

The two possible outcomes in a Bernoulli trial are called 'success' (which occurs with probability p) and 'failure' (which occurs with probability q). p + q must add up to 1. Bernoulli trials are like tossing coins, except the probabilities p and q are not usually equal to 1/2.

Suppose you are conducting a Bernoulli trial where n (the number of trials) is 5 and the probability p of success on any one trial is 2/3. If you are not familiar with how notation is used for probabilities, read through Chapter 8. To find out the probability of having exactly two successes we use the formula:

$$P(k \text{ successes}) = C(n, k)p^k q^{n-k}$$

where P is the probability, k is any number between 0 and n, n is the number of trials and C means 'combine' the figures in brackets (see page 181 for how to combine probabilities).

Step 1. Work out the values for the variables: $k = 2$, $n = 5$, $p = 2/3$ and $q = 1/3$.

Step 2. $P(2 \text{ successes}) = C(5, 2)(2/3)^2 (1/3)^3$
$$= (10 \times 4) \div 3^5$$
$$= 40 \div 3^5$$
$$= 0.1646$$

There is a probability of 0.1646 of having exactly 2 successes.

Binomial distribution

The formula we have just used gives a binomial distribution for the probabilities and can be used to solve the following problem. Suppose your company is marketing a new brand of shampoo. You post a sample sachet of the shampoo to a large number of households and after a few weeks you begin to telephone a sample of these households to ask if they have bought your shampoo after receiving the free sachet. Let's call the number of people who say yes to this question x. So far, you have telephoned 4 people – call this number n. Each telephone call is an 'independent trial' because, we assume, each person's response has not been influenced by any of the other people's responses. Each person that you telephone answers either yes or no to your question, and we assume that each person is equally likely to answer yes.

In this kind of situation we will have a 'binomial distribution' for x, the number of yes answers. You decide to make an analysis of the sample data after making four telephone calls. The possible numbers of yes answers you can get are 0, 1, 2, 3 and 4. These are the only possible values of x.

Suppose the probability of any one person in your sample saying yes is 1 in 4, or 0.25, and the probability of that person saying no is 3 in 4, or 0.75. These values of p and q can be inserted into the binomial formula to find the probabilities of x taking each of its possible values. You will arrive at:

$$P(x = 0) = 1 \times 0.25^0 \times 0.75^4 = 0.316$$
$$P(x = 1) = 4 \times 0.25 \times 0.75^3 = 0.422$$
$$P(x = 2) = 6 \times 0.25^2 \times 0.75^2 = 0.211$$
$$P(x = 3) = 4 \times 0.25^3 \times 0.75 = 0.047$$
$$P(x = 4) = 1 \times 0.25^4 \times 0.75^0 = 0.004$$

Fortunately, a large number of binomial trials approximate a normal distribution and the tests in this chapter can be used to calculate confidence intervals for the value of p.

Conclusion

Understanding the theory behind sampling is the key to using statistics: more often than not, it is inevitable that you will use a sample rather than take a census of the whole population. Hypothesis testing is a rigorous way of making sure that you make the right assumptions about the data, and needs to be applied to the design of any 'experiment' that you make on the data. There is a multiplicity of tests that can be used, but a flow chart can help you decide which ones are appropriate. This chapter has been an introduction to the complex world of sampling; if you want to become an expert in it, you will need to take a course in the subject.

3

Charts: presenting the data

You've taken your samples, conducted your surveys, done your statistical tests, calculated your regressions, and now you have to put your information into a form that other people can understand easily.

In this chapter we will look at ways in which to present this information. Presenting information clearly requires some thought; if you charge ahead and produce a lengthy table, for example, it's quite possible that the only person who will ever read it is you. The first thing to do is to identify exactly why you want to present the information, and secondly to consider who is going to read it and why.

If you are going to include a set of data in a report, you probably have one of two reasons for doing so:

1 *Information for demonstration.* You want to show why a statement is so, or to give evidence that supports your argument. This is the most common reason for including data.

2 *Information for reference.* You want to provide numerical information that other people are going to refer to and extract figures from in order to make further analyses.

These are two slightly different things, and you should take care to distinguish between them in your own mind. Essentially, it is the difference between reporting facts and making interpretations based on facts. Facts are true or false, but interpretations are often more ambiguous, so you need to be able to show exactly how you have made your interpretation so other people can check it, and, possibly, offer a different interpretation that is equally valid, or raises questions that you have not answered.

What's the best way to present data for demonstration?

In general, if you are making a face-to-face presentation, you will nearly always use simplified summaries of numerical information in chart form for demonstration purposes only. This is because most people find it difficult to follow complex numerical information at meetings and lectures, even if they are perfectly able to do the sums for themselves in the privacy of their own offices and homes. It is good practice, therefore, to tell people where they can obtain the full information so they can check it for themselves (this can be in the form of a note on a slide or a handout), but to stick to providing the overall gist of the information in the presentation. The key here is that the summary should accurately reflect the detailed information: very often, presenters give false or misleading summaries because they have jumped to conclusions about the data.

When producing written work, if you are planning to refer to more than two or three numbers in a single paragraph, you are usually better off presenting the information as a chart or a table rather than burying them in your sentences. The readers of your reports are likely to want the numbers to be easy to follow. This means that you should use charts or tables when dealing with numbers, because they are far easier for the reader to take in.

Always have a paragraph accompanying the chart or table which explains what it means. They may be obvious to you, but, generally, charts and tables don't speak for themselves. The paragraph should make not more than three or four points, all of which are clearly related to the information in the chart or table.

Use tables to show quantities

It is best to use tables when you want to draw attention to specific numbers. For example, if you want to say that the number of sales staff has increased from 2,500 in 14 territories in 2005 to 12,000 in 31 territories in 2010, it is better to use a table, which might include numbers for the intervening years too. Your readers can refer to the table and do quick sums in their heads, confident that the numbers are right.

Use charts to compare things

If the points you are making are comparative and don't rely on specific numbers, use a chart. Points like: 'there is a downward trend'; 'the percentage of customers in the public sector has increased sharply'; or 'C2s eat fish and chips more often than Cls', need a chart. Charts usually take more time to prepare than tables, so when choosing between them, err on the side of tables. They also take up more space on the page. A small, unreadable chart is worse than nothing at all, so if you don't have much space, use a table.

Using tables to demonstrate data

Here are the key points to remember when preparing a table for demonstration purposes:

- Round the numbers heavily to make them easier to follow. It's usually best to present numbers in tables correct to two significant figures.
- If you want your readers to compare certain numbers with one another, put the numbers in a column rather than in a row.
- Think about the order in which the rows and/or columns of your table should appear; some orders are easier to read than others.
- When you can, give totals and averages for columns and rows to help the reader.
- Make sure that you have a paragraph explaining the table as close as possible to it on the page. This helps readers to check that they have read the table correctly.
- Keep your tables small; it is much better to have four or five tables demonstrating particular points than to have one big table which no one, except you, will be bothered to read. Don't waste people's time by making things harder to understand than they need to be.

Tables for reference data

Make sure that reference tables are easy for the reader to use; they should be easy to read and the data must be carefully defined. Ensure that:

- All the information that the reader needs to understand the table is included. State what kind of things are being enumerated, the units of measurement used, the period of time the data cover and the source of the data.
- Space the columns and rows equally, and separate averages and totals by lines to make them easy to read. If you do this, you shouldn't usually need to separate each column and row by vertical and horizontal lines.
- If a table doesn't fit on one page, repeat the row and column headings on each page.

■ Keep your categories the same throughout the table; for instance, don't change categories from one time period to the next.

■ Put the categories which will be compared most often in columns; reading up and down a column is easier than across a row.

1   A survey produces the following results. Assuming that the figures of 60% and 40% in the chart are correct, what is misleading about the chart?

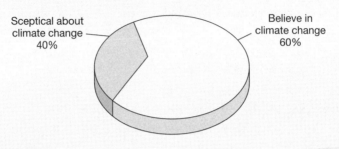

Sceptical about
climate change
40%

Believe in
climate change
60%

Figure 3.1   Survey results

2   What is misleading about this bar chart of house prices?

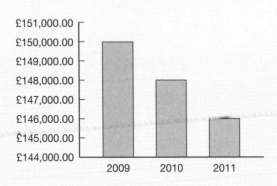

Figure 3.2   Average house prices

See page 203 for the answers.

Using charts

As mentioned earlier, charts and graphs are almost always used to demonstrate points rather than to present reference data. In some cases, you could provide reference data in the form of a chart or graph, but it is slow and awkward to read off the numbers.

The advantages of charts over tables are:

- They are nice to look at, and break up the page. They help to make a report pleasant to read.
- People who don't like numbers find them easy to understand.
- It is much easier to show trends graphically than as a table.
- They make points about comparisons very directly.

The disadvantages are:

- Sophisticated charts are easily misinterpreted by the general reader.
- They can be expensive to prepare.
- It is hard to show specific numbers clearly on a chart.

When constructing a chart, the first thing to remember is that the simpler it is, the better it is. Ask yourself who will see the chart, and what the main points are that you want the viewers to understand. Will they be ready to read the chart carefully, or will they expect to understand it at a glance? The purpose of a chart is to make information easy to understand by putting it in a visual form; make sure that your chart actually achieves this.

Figure 3.3 shows examples of the right and wrong uses of charts. Chart A is taken from sales literature; because it has no scale, it is not possible to know what it means. Making the lines A, B and C three dimensional may look pretty, but it doesn't help us understand what is meant. Chart B, on the other hand, shows the population of a country organised by age and sex; it conveys a lot of information at a glance, and further study will reveal even more.

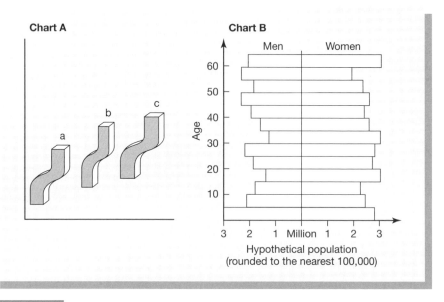

Figure 3.3   **The right and wrong use of charts**

Three-dimensional charts

Three-dimensional charts may look pretty, but they are harder to read accurately than two-dimensional charts. Take a look at Figure 3.4.

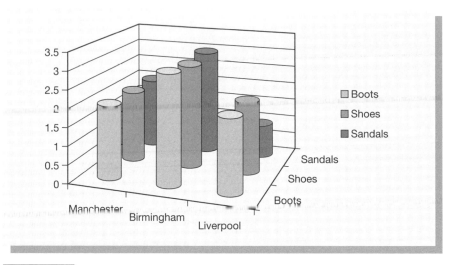

Figure 3.4   A three-dimensional chart for footwear sales

Can you tell from Figure 3.4 which type of footwear was the bigger seller in Birmingham? Was it sandals? You could certainly spend a long time puzzling over it. Now look at Figure 3.5.

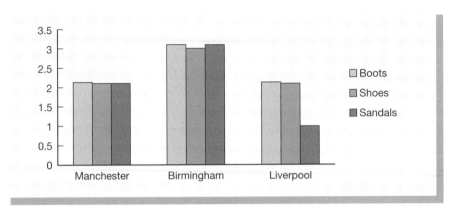

Figure 3.5   Footwear sales as a bar chart

In Figure 3.5 you can see at a glance that boots and sandals were jointly the biggest sellers in Birmingham.

Converting the data to a chart

Before drawing the chart, you must sort and categorise your data so that you clarify your own idea of how the chart should look. Here's a preparation checklist:

1 Collect the data.

2 Check that the data are correct.

3 Sort and categorise the data.

Then, if necessary, you can:

4 Convert the data to standard units.

5 Combine elements.

6 Round small values.

▧ Note the probable size of error and how you have rounded the figures.

▧ State how the data have been collected and compiled.

Rounding (see page 198) is important; trying to keep all the numbers exact is counter-productive if the resulting chart is hard to understand. Chart B in Figure 3.3 rounds to the nearest 100,000 on the horizontal scale – notice that it informs the reader of this fact. Greater accuracy would mean that the chart would have to be much wider.

If you are working from complex tables, watch out for:

1 Irregular intervals, such as certain years missing.

2 Incorrect addition – check the totals for yourself.

3 Figure given in different units, for example, feet and metres. Decide which unit you are going to use, and convert all the data to those units.

4 Footnotes – these often reveal problems with the data.

Choosing the data

Suppose you want to draw a chart for the following information:

Wheat sales in tons	
1940	1,275,340
1950	2,351,910
1960	3,109,250
1970	2,550,680
1980	3,627,250

One of the reasons you want to draw the chart is that you want people to notice that the 1970 figure is double the one for 1940, and that the difference between the figures for 1940 and 1950 is the same as the difference between 1970 and 1980. Figure 3.6 shows some of the ways you could display this information.

In Figure 3.6, Chart 1 shows the general trend of sales, but doesn't reveal the differences in value very clearly. Chart 2, a bar chart, is probably the best way to show the differences, and also gives an idea of the trend, Chart 3 is a pie chart; it expresses values as a proportion of the total, and gives no indication of trends – you would probably rule this one out immediately. Chart 4 is a pictorial chart, which turns the bar chart on its side and replaces the bars with pictures of sheaves of wheat, which helps readers to focus on the subject matter. Notice that each sheaf of wheat represents 500,000 tons. For our example, a bar chart (Chart 2) is generally the best choice, while the pictorial chart (Chart 4) may be effective for audiences not familiar with the subject matter.

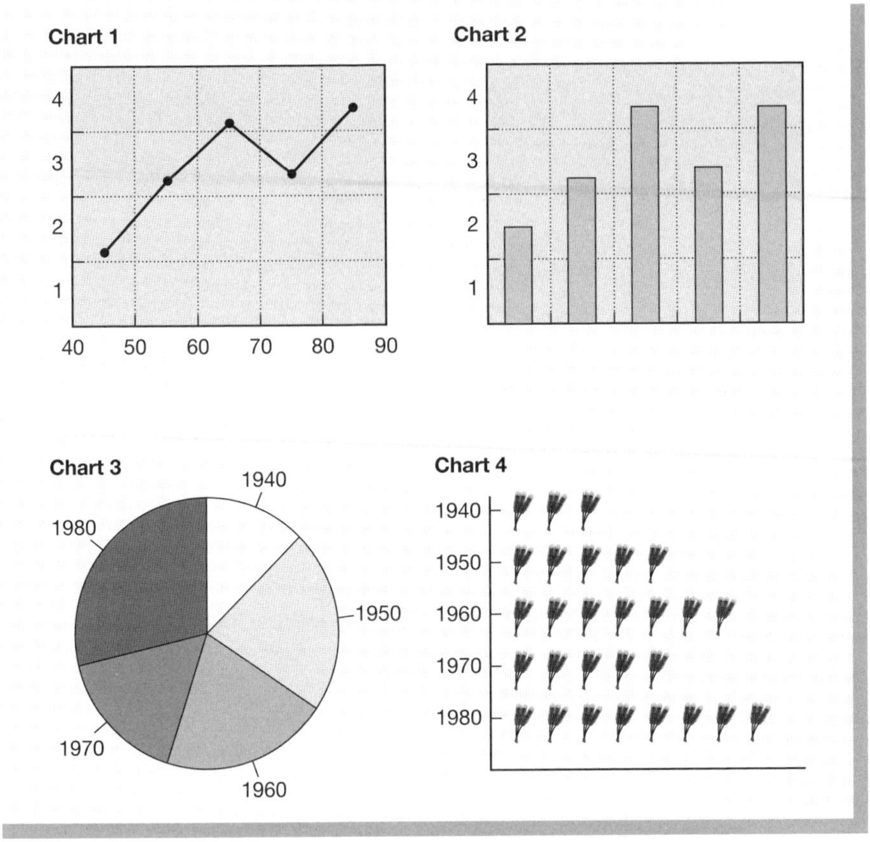

Figure 3.6 Four ways to chart wheat sales

Scales

The scale of a chart can cause a lot of confusion. People tend to think that scales are linear and in proportion, but a surprising number are logarithmic (see page 200).

Figure 3.7 illustrates the point; while the horizontal scale is a normal linear scale with each decade given an equal length, the vertical scale is logarithmic. A cursory glance at the graph might lead you to think that the value rose by approximately the same amount in each half century, but in fact it is multiplied by the same (unknown) factor in each half century.

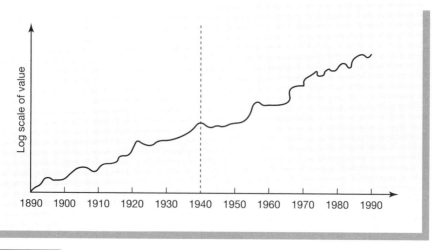

Figure 3.7   Logarithmic chart of value over time

Log scales help to get all the figures on one page, but you must make sure that your readers are aware that you are using such scales if you don't want to confuse them. If you do have a category or a value that is vastly different from the rest, try indicating it pictorially as in Figure 3.8, rather than using a log scale.

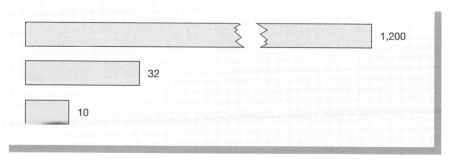

Figure 3.8   How to incorporate an extreme value in a bar chart

Real-life stories   **Misleading log scales in real life: drug dosage**

Recently a well-known pharmaceutical company was criticised for producing
misleading graphical information about a proprietary painkiller in order to defend
it against claims that it was addictive. By using a graph similar to Figure 3.9,
salespeople attempted to persuade doctors that the painkiller was not particularly
addictive; the graph appeared to show that the amount of the drug in the
bloodstream stays on a plateau for many hours.

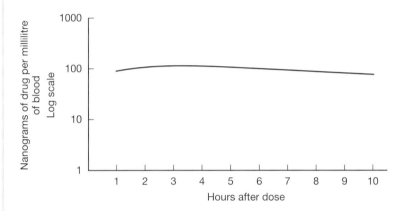

Figure 3.9   Effects of drug dosage, log scale on vertical axis

However, when the same data were plotted using a linear scale (see Figure 3.10),
the picture was different.

Figure 3.10   Effects of drug dosage, linear scale on both axes

Figure 3.10 shows the drug building up to a peak after 2–3 hours before dropping off
quite rapidly. This effect, say the critics, may make patients feel that the drug is wearing
off, leading them to take another dose, and, eventually, to addictive behaviour.

More on bar charts

Bar charts are extremely useful for illustrating statistical information, but making them crystal clear takes some thought. For example, dividing bars to show proportions can cause difficulties. Check these points:

- that all the values are in the same units;
- that the values add up to the total;
- that you will be able to label the largest and smallest values;
- that the smallest values are not going to be too small to read clearly.

The person who drew the pictorial chart in Figure 3.11 wanted to show that D and F were equal in value, and hoped that this was clear because it was indicated on the vertical scale. Readers might well think that F is bigger than D, however, because F uses up more of the horizontal dimension of the picture. A, B and C are too small to make sense; it would be much better to draw a conventional bar chart.

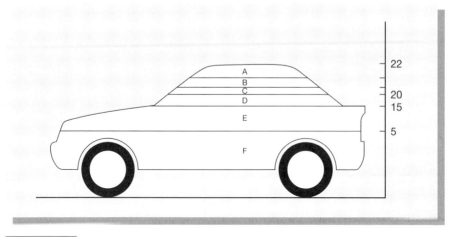

| Figure 3.11 | A misleading pictorial bar chart |

Pie charts

Pie charts are best used when you have no more than five categories with a small spread. If you have many categories with a few extreme values, you will end up in a mess. To draw the proportions accurately, you will need a protractor to measure the angles, or use PC software. Here's how to convert your data into degrees:

Step 1. Convert all your categories to the same units.

Step 2. Add the values of the categories together and divide by 100.

Step 3. Divide the value of each category by the result of step 2 and express it as a percentage.

Step 4. Multiply each percentage by 3.6 to convert to degrees.

Step 5. Check that the percentages for the different categories add up to 100 and that the degrees add up to 360.

Which chart to use?

Decide which kind of chart to use by considering what kind of comparison you want to illustrate. Here's a list of comparisons and the appropriate chart for each:

- Different elements as part of a whole – use pie charts for preference, or else a bar chart.
- Changes in the composition of a whole – use pie charts or bar charts.
- The frequency of different measurements – use bar charts.
- The way related measurements, or a single measurement, change over time – use a line graph, or else a bar chart.
- The correlation of variables – use a scattergram.

Summary: general rules for drawing charts

Here are the basic rules to follow when using charts in reports and presentations:

- Always plan your chart before you start.
- Always include clear explanations of the kinds of things that are being represented, the scales of measurement, the units used and the source of the information. In many cases you should also state the period of time that the data covers and the geographical area from which the data was obtained.
- Try to make the chart as easy as possible to read; don't make it too big or too small. Try to label the chart directly rather than referring the reader to a complicated key or set of symbols. If you are using line shading to distinguish between different elements, especially on a

single-colour chart, make sure that it is easy to see the difference between the shadings at a glance.

- Make sure that your chart is easy to understand at first glance. Always include an explanation of the chart in the text.

- If you have a lot of information to show in the chart, break it up into two or three simpler charts.

- If it is essential to show a chart of a kind that will be unfamiliar to your readers, carefully explain how to understand it in the text. For instance, if you are using a logarithmic scale, give an example of how a familiar measurement would look on a logarithmic scale.

4

Forecasting: time series analysis and regression analysis

This fascinating subject has many effective rules and methodologies. No honest forecaster will pretend that any prediction about the future is 100% certain to occur, and will emphasise that good forecasts are simply educated guesses that may change in the light of new information. This chapter looks at the following topics and techniques.

- What is a forecast?
- Extrapolation.
- Judgement, guesses and indicators.
- Leading indicators.
- Time series.
- The multiplicative time series model.
- Regression analysis.
- A new development: Reference Class Forecasting

What is a forecast?

In its broadest sense, a forecast is a statement made by someone about the future. It may be based on sound reasoning and calculations, or educated guesses, or be simply plucked out of thin air. There is a huge range of fore- casting methods; the best method to use depends upon the kind of thing you are attempting to forecast. While most organisations reject methods like astrology and card reading on the grounds that there is no substantial evidence that they work, and have a tendency to prefer elaborate, mathematically based methods, it is important to recognise that these techniques, too, often depend on making assumptions that may simply turn out to be wrong. In business, there is a danger of becoming overly impressed by the 'false precision' of complex, professional-seeming forecasts in situations that do not lend themselves to accurate forecasting; for example, the outcomes of wars, prices in the stock markets, and many macroeconomic events, are notoriously difficult to forecast.

When thinking about forecasts, we should recognise that it is generally easier to anticipate short-term events, say, up to a year ahead, than medium-term events (say, one to five years), or long-term events (five years or more). Even the definitions of 'medium term' and 'long term' can be problematic; some forecasters regard anything over two years as 'long term', for example. Also, there is an important difference between knowing that an event is likely to occur at some time in the future, and being able to forecast precisely when it will happen. For example, scientists are fairly sure that at some time in the far future the planets of the solar system will no longer exist, but estimates of when this may occur vary by billions of years.

One way of dealing with the problem of imprecision is to describe the distribution of probable outcomes around a central point denoting the most probable outcome. Thus, the Bank of England, for instance, publishes charts of projected inflation that illustrate a range of possible inflation rates that widens as they progress further into the future; in its estimates produced in February 2011,[1] for example, the range of estimates increases from approximately 3%–6% two quarters ahead, to between –0.5% and just under 5% by the end of 2013. This widening of the range indicates the increase in uncertainty the further we look into the future.

Many people in both the private and public sectors are under pressure to make overly confident forecasts. There is a massive demand for forecasts, as any doctor, stockbroker, economist or politician will tell you. The problem is that many people, including many media organisations, don't want to hear an honest forecast, which should most often be 'well, we can't be sure, but . . .'. This demand for overly confident forecasts is met by a large number of specialised organisations and individuals who are willing to supply them, relying on the fact that in many cases nobody minds much if the forecast is not accurate. There's an old story which sheds some light on why this is so: when some army officers try to resign from a forecasting

[1] *Inflation Report February 2011*, Bank of England, Chart 5.1, p. 40.

assignment because they cannot get their predictions right, they are told, 'the General knows your forecasts are wrong, but he needs them for planning purposes'.

Extrapolation

Extrapolation means estimating future values on the assumption that current trends will continue. It is reasonable to make short-term forecasts using extrapolation in situations where existing tendencies have persisted for a long time. For example, if you have a customer who has purchased 500 pounds' worth of goods from you every week for the past 150 weeks, it might not be unreasonable to forecast that the customer will purchase 500 pounds' worth of goods from you every week for the next four weeks, all other things being equal. However, the further you extrapolate into the future, the more likely it becomes that new factors will emerge that change the trend, so your forecasts are likely to become less accurate. For example, if house prices have risen every year by the same rate for the past 10 years, it would be unwise to forecast the price of your house in seven years' time by simple extrapolation, because the forces driving house prices may alter during the intervening period. Suppose the housing market crashes two years in the future and then stagnates for five years; your prediction of seven years might then be way off.

Professional forecasters often try to measure the effectiveness of a method of forecasting by testing it against a benchmark of 'naïve extrapolation', which means a simple extrapolation as described above. In a given situation, if a forecasting method is less inaccurate than a forecast by naïve extrapolation, then it is regarded as a more accurate method; this is a reasonable approach, but it is worth noting that simply because a forecasting method is better than extrapolation, it does not necessarily mean that it is a reliable forecasting method, especially in the medium to long term.

Judgement, guesses and indicators

Many forecasts incorporate judgements, and even outright guesses, into their methods. For example, in the Delphi method, a range of experts are given a series of questionnaires asking them to make predictions about the future; they are told the results of each questionnaire before the next one, and are invited to revise their opinions, the idea being to obtain some kind of consensus. The method was developed by the RAND corporation in the 1960s as a way of trying to get experts to produce predictions about future military technology that most of them could agree upon, and has subsequently been used remarkably widely by large organisations, with mixed results. As a method of trying to get experts to agree on something it may be very valuable, but as a forecasting method there are some obvious problems. For example, since the experts are basically using their judgement, or guessing, why should encouraging them to modify their forecasts towards a consensus make the forecasts any more accurate? And why should we believe that someone who has great expertise in a subject should be good at making forecasts, especially about matters that are inherently difficult to forecast in the long term? The continued use of the Delphi method may tell us more about the need for bureaucracies to have some kind of forecast to hang on to, than about the method's success at generating accurate predictions. Experts are experts about the present and the past, not about the future.

Another forecasting method relies on the use of 'indicators', a term used in economics to refer to certain statistics that are regarded as important. There are 'leading', 'coincident' and 'lagging' indicators, classified according to where they are supposed to appear in the business cycle (the 'business cycle' itself being a rather nebulous concept). 'Leading indicators', which are thought to change before the economy as a whole changes, are sometimes used to make short-term predictions. For example, the stock market is often seen as a leading indicator of the 'real economy' as a whole, because the stock market tends to rise or fall some time before the real economy. And the number of builders beginning to build houses is a pretty good leading indicator of the number of buildings that are going to be finished in the future. But even when the relationship between the leading indicator and the thing it is supposed to lead is fairly clear, as with housing starts and finished houses, we can't predict the time of the lag precisely; for example, if there is a period of very bad weather, or builders suddenly find it hard to borrow money, or nobody wants to buy houses, the length of time between housing starts and their completion will increase substantially.

Real-life stories   Leading indicators in real life

Although economic indicators are useful tools when used intelligently, they are also a major source of false precision in forecasts. Furthermore, some models using a collection of leading indicators have had some success during normal conditions, but have completely failed to forecast unusual critical events – this is undesirable, because it is the rare, disastrous event that we would most like to be able to forecast so that we can take steps to minimise our losses. Here are two examples to illustrate the issues.

Researchers in the US studied two complex models based on weighted indices of leading indicators; one produced by the US Commerce Department, and another by two well-known economists, James Stock and Mark Watson. During the 1980s, both the Commerce Department and the Stock-Watson indices had been quite good at predicting economic performance two quarters ahead, although they did considerably worse at predicting four quarters ahead. In 1990–91, when there was a major recession following the surprise Iraqi invasion of Kuwait, both indices produced completely inaccurate forecasts.

Another study in South Africa found that the FNB/BER Consumer Confidence Index, based on consumer surveys, and the South African Reserve Bank Leading Indicator, a complex index based on a group of indicators, were not the reliable forecasting tools they had hitherto been assumed to be, but for slightly different reasons. In the case of the Consumer Confidence Index, it had been claimed that consumer confidence was a good indicator of GDP growth, based on graphs that appeared to show a close correlation between the two; it was less clear, however, whether consumer confidence led or lagged changes in GDP. Statistical analysis found that in fact it was not possible to demonstrate that consumer confidence was not lagging behind GDP, and that the index could not therefore be used legitimately to make forecasts. The researchers pointed out that when you ask consumers about their expectations for the future, they are very likely to extrapolate from current trends, which, as we have already seen, is not a good method of prediction.

In the case of Reserve Bank's Leading Indicator index, it had been widely assumed during the 1980s and 1990s that the index was a good predictor of changes in growth trends in the South African economy. Again, this assumption was based on charts that appeared to show that the index led changes in economic growth, but in-depth statistical tests established that it was actually lagging behind changes in economic growth, and, therefore, could not be used to predict them. In 2004 the bank adjusted the components of the index in an effort to increase the lead time, but the researchers argued that it had failed to apply the appropriate statistical tests to establish the truth of this claim.

Time series

Now that we have considered some of the limitations of forecasting, we can look at one of the main approaches to making sense of trends in business data: time series. A time series is simply a series of measurements taken at different times. For example, you can produce a time series for the rate of inflation each quarter, or for your company's sales each month. In many organisations, data about their business are much more meaningful when they are compared with figures for different periods. You can display time series in the form of a graph in order to get a general idea of what is happening, or else tabulate it in order to examine it closely.

The two main reasons why time series are useful are:

1   You can examine past and present performance to see if it is better or worse than expected. To do this, seasonal variations and long-term factors may have to be taken into account.

2   You can use time series to try to predict future performance. No one can predict the future, so what you have to say is, 'if the pattern of the future is similar to the pattern of the past, then you can predict that . . .'. Usually, future performance doesn't exactly resemble past performance, but examining the difference between actual performance and predicted performance can sometimes reveal the cause of the difference.

You can use time series analysis to try to predict overall demand for a product in a market, the future cost of materials, or future sales. Estimating future sales accurately is vital in business, because so many other plans are based upon sales forecasts. There are a great many ways to analyse time series; we shall look at just one.

The multiplicative time series model

This horrible-sounding name refers to a way of representing time series data by taking four factors, or components, into account; the *secular trend*, the *seasonal indices*, the *long-term cycle* and *irregular fluctuation*. We shall look at each of these factors separately before looking at an example.

Secular trend (T)

A secular trend is a tendency for a time series to show a pattern of increase or decrease for a year or more. For example, the population of the US has grown fairly steadily since the war, so the trend is for growth. The secular trend is also called the 'long-term' trend.

Seasonal indices (S)

The seasonal index gives a number to the tendency for a time series to follow a seasonal pattern. A famous example is ice-cream sales: you tend to sell more ice cream when it is hot. Remember, though, that many time series don't have a seasonal pattern, for instance, petrol sales and bond prices.

Much of the data that is published about the economy, such as the unemployment figures, are adjusted for seasonal variations. Seasonal variations don't have to be the four seasons of the year – they could be patterns within a week, or even a day. In cities, there are times of the day when the roads are jammed with cars, and other times when the roads are empty; this is an example of a 'seasonal variation' during a single day.

A seasonal index is a number which describes a tendency in a particular period of time, say a monthly or a quarter, to be higher than other periods of equal length at other times of the year. Time series for quarterly reports will have four seasonal indices, while time series for monthly reports will have 12 indices. Seasonal indices are usually a number near 1.0. If you adjust the secular trend by multiplying it by the seasonal index, your forecast will tend to be improved:

Sales forecast = Seasonal index × Secular trend forecast

Long-term cycles (C)

The long-term cycle describes variations that are due to conditions lasting longer than one or two years. This is not very long, you might think, but it indicates the great difficulty of making accurate forecasts more than one or two years ahead.

In terms of business, a long-term cycle usually means the effect of prosperity or recession on such things as prices, unemployment and retail sales.

Irregular fluctuations (I)

An irregular fluctuation means any variation that none of the other three terms can explain. It is present in almost all time series, and tends to make the other components more difficult to spot; we use a special method to remove it.

Figure 4.1 shows what the graphs of different components of the same time series might look like. The model assumes that these four components, or 'terms', when multiplied together will represent the value of any observation in a time series. In other words, if we call the observation 'y', y is given by the formula:

$$y = T \times S \times C \times I$$

where T is the secular trend for the period, S is the seasonal index for the period, C is the long-term cycle for the period and I is the irregular fluctuation for the period.

The next step is to find out how the terms are identified. We will illustrate the techniques with an example. Suppose that a company's quarterly sales figures over three years are as shown (in thousands) in Table 4.1.

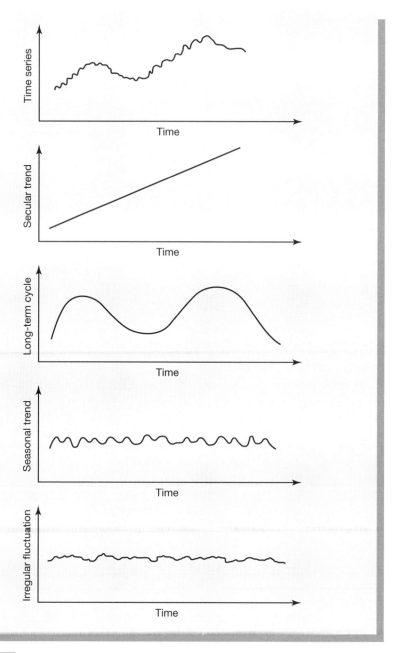

Figure 4.1   The components of a time series

Table 4.1 Company's sale figures over three years

	First quarter	Second quarter	Third quarter	Fourth quarter
1993	42	52	55	42
1994	45	60	67	52
1995	64	81	85	66

Figure 4.2 shows these figures plotted on a graph.

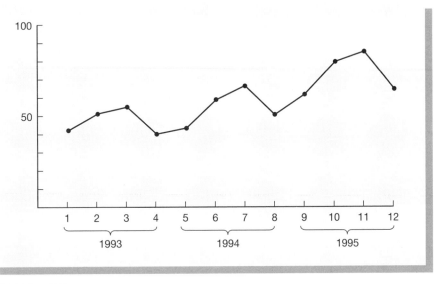

Figure 4.2   Graph of quarterly sales from Table 4.1

Finding the secular trend

The easiest of the four components to find is usually the secular trend. One way to find it is by linear regression, using the least squares method (see page 90 for a more detailed explanation of how this works). The aim here is to calculate and plot a line that best 'fits' the observations.

Using Figure 4.2, add all the values of the observations on the y axis (the vertical axis) together to get the sum of y; the sum is 711. Then add all the values of the observations on the x axis (the horizontal axis) together to find the sum of x, which is 78. The means of x and y are therefore:

$$\bar{y} = 711 \div 12 = 59.25$$

and

$$\bar{x} = 78 \div 12 = 6.5$$

Next, we compute the sum of the squares of each time value, which is written as Σx^2. Square each of your time values and then add the squares:

	First quarter	Second quarter	Third quarter	Fourth quarter
	$1 \times 1 = 1$	$2 \times 2 = 4$	$3 \times 3 = 9$	$4 \times 4 = 16$
	$5 \times 5 = 25$	$6 \times 6 = 36$	$7 \times 7 = 49$	$8 \times 8 = 64$
	$9 \times 9 = 81$	$10 \times 10 = 100$	$11 \times 11 = 121$	$12 \times 12 = 144$
Total	107	140	179	224

$$\Sigma x^2 = 650$$

Now we compute the sum of the products of the x and y values, written as Σxy. Multiply the value of each observation of x and y together and then add them all together:

	$42 \times 1 = 42$	$52 \times 2 = 104$	$55 \times 3 = 165$	$42 \times 4 = 168$
	$45 \times 5 = 225$	$60 \times 6 = 360$	$67 \times 7 = 469$	$52 \times 8 = 416$
	$64 \times 9 = 576$	$81 \times 10 = 810$	$85 \times 11 = 935$	$66 \times 12 = 792$
Total	843	1,274	1,569	1,376

$$\Sigma xy = 5,062$$

Next, we calculate certain quantities, conventionally called Sxx and Syy, that are related to the variance and covariance of the x and y values:

$$S_{xx} = \Sigma x^2 - n\bar{x}^2$$
$$S_{yy} = \Sigma x^2 - n\bar{y}^2$$

where n is the number of observations.

We next compute these quantities as:

$$S_{xx} = \Sigma x^2 - n\bar{x}^2 = 650 - (12 \times 6.5^2) = 650 - 507 = 143$$
$$S_{xy} = \Sigma xy - n\bar{x}\bar{y} = 5,062 - (12 \times 6.5 \times 59.62) = 440.5$$

We express the line we want using the formula:

$$y = a + bx$$

where

$$b = Sxy \div Sxx$$
$$a = y - bx$$

We can work out that b, the slope of the line, is:

$$b = Sxy \div Sxx = 440.5 \div 143 = 3.08$$

and a is:

$$a = y - bx = 59.25 - (3.08 \times 6.5) = 59.25 - 20.02 = 39.23$$

Thus the equation for the line is:

$$y = 39.23 + 3.08x$$

Figure 4.3 shows this line drawn through the graph of sales figures shown previously in Figure 4.2.

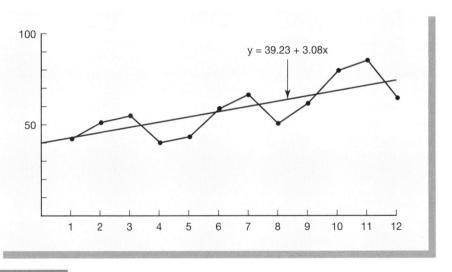

Figure 4.3   Graph of the secular trend in quarterly sales

This method of calculating the secular trend works if the underlying trend is linear. Sometimes, though, it is necessary to find a curve, or to weight more recent observations more heavily to try to show the effect of more recent trends. Many of these methods are too complicated to be covered in this book, but we can look at one of the simpler techniques, which is the use of 'exponential growth curves'.

Exponential growth curves for secular trends

If you have a time series that is growing by a fixed percentage in each period (not counting unexplained variations), the secular trend is better described by an exponential growth curve; a linear relationship does not give a good fit in the circumstances.

Suppose you deposit £1,000 in a bank with an effective interest rate of 4% a year. The total amount you will have in the account at the end of any particular year can be expressed as 1,000 × (1.04), where n is the number of years; plotted on a graph, these points will be a curve showing exponential growth. You can write this in the general form:

$$y_n = a(1 + r)^n$$

where a is the initial amount, r is the growth rate, n is the number of periods and y is the amount at a chosen period. If you take the logarithms (logs) of the data, the equation looks like this:

$$\log y = \log a + n \log(1 + r)$$

In this situation there is actually a linear relationship between the log of y and the time n (rather than between y itself and n). In situations where you think the secular trend is one of exponential growth, it makes good sense to take the log of the observations y and then try to find the linear relationships for these.

Finding the seasonal variation

Turn back to Figure 4.1. The differences between the points on the graph of the observed quarterly sales figures and the points that are 'predicted' by the secular regression line are called the 'residuals' (see page 93). You can work out the values for the residuals by calculating the predicted value of any observation from the equation of the line and subtracting it from the observed value. The results are shown in Table 4.2.

Table 4.2 Seasonal variation for quarterly sales

Quarter	Observed y	Predicted $\hat{y} = 39.23 + 3.08x$	Residual $y - \hat{y}$
1	42	42.31	−0.31
2	52	45.39	6.61
3	55	48.47	6.53
4	42	51.55	−9.55
5	45	54.63	−9.63
6	60	57.71	2.29
7	67	60.79	6.21
8	52	63.87	−11.87
9	64	66.95	−2.95
10	81	70.03	10.97
11	85	73.11	11.89
12	66	76.19	−10.19

The residuals show that the predictions are always too high in the first and last quarters of the year and too low in the second and third quarters. This means that the residuals are 'serially correlated'.

You can summarise this by taking the results in pairs; if you pair quarters 1 and 2, 3 and 4, and so on, you would have a serial correlation of 'lag 1'. If you paired 1 and 3, 2 and 4, and so on, you have a serial correlation of 'lag 2'. If you paired 1 and 4, 2 and 5, and so on, there would be a lag of 3, and a lag 4 would be for the pairs I and 5, 2 and 6, and so on. The pairs with lag 4 are actually the corresponding quarters in each year; we might well expect to find a seasonal trend where the corresponding quarters in each year behaved in a similar way.

We can measure the correlation of these pairs by calculating a number called the serial correlation coefficient (r) for each lag time; this is very, very long-winded by hand so we won't do it here. It gives a value for r between 1 and −1.

Here are the residuals from our example, arranged in pairs with lag 4:

Pair 1 and 5	−0.31	−9.63
Pair 2 and 6	6.61	2.29
Pair 3 and 7	6.53	6.21
Pair 4 and 8	−9.55	−11.87
Pair 5 and 9	−9.63	−2.95
Pair 6 and 10	2.29	10.97
Pair 7 and 11	6.21	11.89
Pair 8 and 12	−11.87	−10.19

The last pair we can make is 8 and 12, since we only have 12 quarterly observations to work with. Figure 4.4 shows a graph called a 'correlogram' which plots r values for each lag on the y axis and the lags on the x axis using imaginary data.

The correlogram shows lags 4 and 8 with high positive correlations (their r values are near 1); this makes it clear that if the data were of quarterly sales figures, it would mean that the corresponding quarters in each year were highly correlated, and there was indeed a seasonal trend.

If you plot large numbers of lags, you might well find correlations that you would not have otherwise noticed.

Seasonal indices

We saw earlier that seasonal indices are numbers that reflect the tendency for the observation in a period to be higher or lower than other periods in the year. Having decided on the length of the seasonal variation, we group together all the data that occur in the same 'season'. In our case, we have identified a seasonal variation of length 1 year, so we group together all the first quarter results to compute a first quarter seasonal index, all the second quarter results to compute a second quarter seasonal index, and so on for the third and fourth quarter indices.

To see how the index number is calculated, let's look at Table 4.3 which shows the sales figures for the first quarter for each of the three years in the example and the ratio between the observed figure and the number predicted by the regression line.

Table 4.3 First quarter sales figures (1993, 1994, 1995)

	Observed	Predicted	Observed/predicted
1993	42	42.31	0.9926
1994	45	54.63	0.8237
1995	64	66.95	0.9559

These ratios might be being influenced by long-term cycles and irregular fluctuations. These effects can be reduced by taking the mean average of the ratios to be the index:

$$\text{1st quarter index} = (0.9926 + 0.8237 + 0.9559) \div 3$$
$$= 2.7722 \div 3$$
$$= 0.9241$$

If you had some values for first quarters which were far different from the rest, you could choose the median average as the index instead. The seasonal index for the first quarter can be written as S_1.

In a similar way, we compute the second, third and fourth quarter indices as:

$$S_2 = (1.1456 + 1.0396 + 1.1566) \div 3 = 1.1139$$
$$S_3 = (1.1347 + 1.1021 + 1.1626) \div 3 = 1.1331$$
$$S_4 = (0.8147 + 0.8141 + 0.8662) \div 3 = 0.8317$$

Forecasting with the seasonal index

So far, we have seen how to find the secular trend T, and the seasonal index S. These are the most important of the four components when you make a forecast.

In the example, we have quarterly data for three years, 1993, 1994 and 1995. Suppose you want to forecast the figure for the first quarter of 1996, which would be the thirteenth period in the series. You can find T with the regression line:

$$Y = 39.23 + 3.08x$$
$$\text{T for period 13} = 39.23 + (3.08 \times 13)$$
$$= 79.27$$

Multiplying T_{13} by the seasonal index for the first quarter S_1, will make this forecast more accurate:

$$T_{13} \times S_1 = 79.27 \times 0.9241 = 73.253$$

Removing the seasonal trend

'Seasonally adjusted' means that the seasonal variation in a time series has been taken out in order for other effects to be clearer. For instance, a country's unemployment figures are often seasonally adjusted.

Seasonal adjustments, or 'deseasonalising' is done by dividing each of the observations in the time series by the appropriate seasonal index. In the example, if you want to seasonally adjust the observed sales for the first quarter in 1995, which is 64, you simply divide by S_1:

$$64 \div S_1 = 64 \div 0.9241 = 69.256$$

To see how this affects comparisons with other periods, we'll deseasonalise the second quarter of 1995: $S_2 = 1.1139$. Now, we deseasonalise:

$$81 \div 1.1139 = 72.717$$

Compare the observed figures with the seasonally adjusted ones in Table 4.4.

Table 4.4 Comparison of observed and seasonally adjusted figures

	Observed	*Deseasonalised*
1st quarter 1995	64	69.256
2nd quarter 1995	81	72.717

Comparing the deseasonalised figures, we can see at a glance that the adjusted increase in the second quarter is only about 5%. Looking at the observed figures, they give a rise of more like 30%.

Finding the long term cycle (C) and the irregular component (I)

If you have found the secular trend (T) and the seasonal index (S), then you can find $C \times I$ by dividing the observed figures by $T \times S$. For example, we can do this for the first quarter of 1995 (period 9):

$$\text{Observed period } 9 = 64$$
$$T_9 = 39.23 + (3.08 \times 9) = 66.95$$
$$S_9 = 0.9241$$
$$C_9 \times I_9 = 64 \div (T_9 \times S_9) = 64 \div 61.8685 = 1.0345$$

If you plotted the C × I points for each period on a graph, you might get a pattern of peaks and troughs spanning more than a year from peak to peak (this is the long-term component), but it would be jagged because of the irregular component. You can take out the irregular component I by means of a 'smoothing' method called the 'moving average'. In our example, we do not have enough data to reliably identify a long-term cycle. None the less we can look at the trend of C × I values and smooth them out as described below. This will be useful for predicting one or two periods ahead.

Calculating the moving average

The moving average is frequently used when analysing time series to 'smooth' the data. Every moving average has a certain 'length', which refers to the number of observations that are being averaged. Thus, if you want to calculate the moving average of length 4 in our example, you must work out the following averages for the observed sales (we call them Y1 to Y12):

First average	$(Y1 + Y2 + Y3 + Y4) \div 4$
Second average	$(Y2 + Y3 + Y4 + Y5) \div 4$
Third average	$(Y3 + Y4 + Y5 + Y6) \div 4$
Fourth average	$(Y4 + Y5 + Y6 + Y7) \div 4$
Fifth average	$(Y5 + Y6 + Y7 + Y8) \div 4$
Sixth average	$(Y6 + Y7 + Y8 + Y9) \div 4$
Seventh average	$(Y7 + Y8 + Y9 + Y10) \div 4$
Eighth average	$(Y8 + Y9 + Y10 + Y11) \div 4$
Ninth average	$(Y9 + Y10 + Y11 + Y12) \div 4$

You have to stop here because you only have 12 observations. You have smoothed the data, but you have few points on your curve. The greater the length of your moving average, the smoother the curve will be. You can probably see why it is called a moving average: the number of observations you are averaging stays the same, but you move along the observations once each time.

Moving averages from C × I

On page 81 we made a prediction for the quarterly sales figure in the thirteenth period by multiplying T_{13} by the seasonal index for the first quarter, S_1:

$$T_{13} \times S_1 = 79.27 \times 0.9241 = 73.253$$

We could refine this further by multiplying the moving average of $C \times I$, of length 3, for the last three periods for which we have actual observations. Call this C_{11}.

To work out $C \times I$ for periods 10, 11 and 12, we first have to work out T and then S. T is shown in Table 4.5.

Table 4.5 T values for periods 10, 11 and 12

Period	T
10	70.03
11	73.11
12	76.19

Working out S takes a bit longer because periods 10, 11 and 12 are the second, third and fourth quarters of 1995. We can work out $T \times S$ and $C \times I$ for the three periods.

Remember that $C \times I$ = observed sales ÷ $(T \times S)$ as in Table 4.6.

Table 4.6 T, S and C × I values for periods 10, 11 and 12

Period	Observation	T	S	C × I
10	81	70.03	1.1139	1.0384
11	85	73.11	1.1331	1.0260
12	66	76.19	0.8317	1.0415

C_{11} is the moving average of the figures we have for $C \times I$, so:

$$C_{11} = (1.0384 + 1.0260 + 1.0415) \div 3$$
$$= 3.1059 \div 3$$
$$= 1.0353$$

Finally, we improve our prediction for the sales figure for period 13:

$$T_{13} \times S_1 \times C_{11} = 79.27 \times 0.9241 \times 1.0353 = 75.839$$

Finding the irregular component I

The irregular component is whatever is left when we take out all the other effects. To find I, we divide C × I (the variation not accounted for by secular and seasonal variation) by C.

Summary of quantitative approaches to forecasting

Multiplicative and additive models

We have now examined all the components of the model in detail, and you should be able to plot graphs from time series with two variables showing the different trends. There is a variation on the multiplicative model called the 'additive model', where the components T, S, C and I are added together rather than multiplied together, but the multiplicative model is usually more appropriate in most business problems. There are also more complex models known as 'multivariate models' for analysing time series where the observations have several variables.

Correlation

Suppose it is your first day in a new managerial job, and several employees come to you to complain that your predecessor unfairly favoured certain individuals when raising salaries. The company's policy is to raise salaries according to carefully measured individual productivity, so the first thing you can do is to compare the percentage increase of individuals' salaries with their productivity.

One way of making this kind of comparison is to look for a linear relationship. Say you take a sample of 25 employees in your department, and in order to make the comparison you plot the data on a graph called a 'scattergram', as in Figure 4.4.

The points on the graph are close to a straight line, which is a sign that there is indeed something like a linear relationship between the two variables, the percentage of salary increase and the measure of productivity.

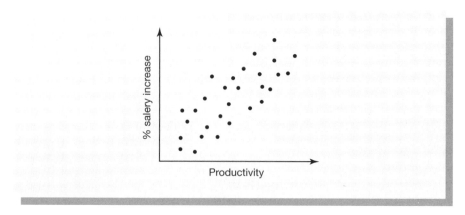

Figure 4.4   Scattergram for salary/productivity

Defining correlation

Going back to Figure 4.4, we can see that although the points tend towards a straight line, they are scattered around it. To measure how much they are scattered around it, we measure the 'strength of the linear relationship'. Measuring the strength of a linear relationship is what is known in statistics as measuring the 'correlation'.

The word 'correlation' is often misunderstood. Statisticians never tire of saying that 'correlation is not causation', which isn't all that helpful, since statistics does not tell us much about what causation is. People naturally want to see a cause and effect relationship in correlation, assuming that the correlation of two events implies that one event causes another event to happen. In statistics, the existence of a correlation is never enough, by itself, to imply a cause and effect relationship. For example, in the 1950s there was a scare in the US that soft drinks were causing polio, because it was found that there were many cases of polio during the time of year when soft drink sales were at their peak. Statistically, polio outbreaks and soft drink consumption were correlated, but it did not mean that drinking soft drinks was causing polio. It was just coincidental that both variables were high during hot weather.

The sample correlation coefficient

Returning to our example in Figure 4.4, we now want to measure the strength of the linear relationship, or correlation, between salary increases and productivity. One way to do this is to calculate the 'sample correlation coefficient', which is written as r, and r is always between 1 and –1. When it is 1, it means that all the points on the graph are on a straight line going up from left to right. When r is –1, all the points on the graph are on a straight line going down from left to right, and if r is close to 0, it means that the points on the graph are very scattered, and are far away from a linear relationship. Figure 4.5 shows r values for various linear relationships.

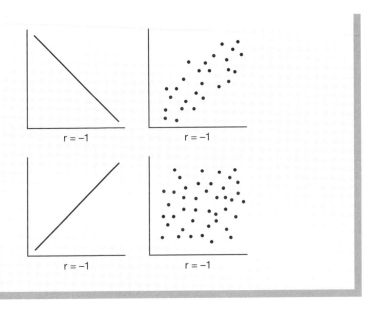

Figure 4.5   r value for various linear relationships

Try to become familiar with r values; you can get yourself to the point where you can look at a scattergram and make a good guess of its r value. You should certainly be able to tell if it is positive or negative, unless r is very close to 0. Now we have learned a little about correlation, we can examine an important technique for analysing and forecasting: regression analysis.

Regression analysis

Regression analysis examines the relationship between two or more variables, and is a powerful forecasting tool.

Suppose your company is in the process of re-examining its pricing structure, and you have been asked to work out how prices affect sales. First you would have to collect information about gross sales and price per unit, and then perform a regression analysis to make a forecast.

To give a more complicated example, suppose you want to sell your house. You have to decide how much to ask for it, and you know that if you set the asking price too high it won't sell, and if you set it too low, it may sell quickly, but you would not get as much money as you could have done. When you are working out how much to ask for, you probably consider the price you paid for it, the general movement of house prices since you bought it, the prices of other houses nearby that have recently been sold, the size of those houses and the amount of land they had, the size of your own house and its land and many other factors. You may find a buyer who falls in love with your house because of its character and will pay over the odds for it, but on average, the kind of information just described will help you to predict how buyers will respond to a particular asking price.

To find a mathematical relationship between all the factors involved in deciding on an asking price is a tough problem, to which regression analysis would be one reasonable solution if you believe that the price is close to being a linear function of all other factors. If you want to make a forecast by analysing the relationship between two variables, the variable you want to forecast is called the 'dependent variable' (written as x) and the variable to which it is related is called the 'independent variable' (written as y).

Linear models

In maths, a model is an equation that represents a relationship. Suppose a gas board charges the labour for repairs at £60 for the first hour's work and £10 for each subsequent quarter of an hour. This could be represented by the equation:

$$y = 60 + 10x$$

where y is the total charged, and x the number of quarter hours after the first hour. Now suppose you selected 5 customers at random and you find the values of x for each of them. Using the equation, it is simple to calculate y:

Customer	1	2	3	4	5
x	4	5	9	1	3
y	100	110	150	70	90

This kind of model is called deterministic, because you can determine the appropriate value of y for any value of x. Since y = 60 + 10x is an equation for a straight line, any customer's charge will fall on that line.

If you were trying to decide on the selling price for your house, though, you wouldn't be able to use a deterministic model. For instance, it wouldn't be very sensible to try to work out the selling price just on the basis of the size of your house, because other factors affect the price, some of which aren't possible to measure.

What you can do, however, is to try to model the relationship with a model that has a deterministic part and a probabilistic part. The deterministic part covers the main features of the relationship and the probabilistic part allows for the variations due to factors that you do not know much about.

For example, suppose you know that pieces of land big enough to build one house on sold for about £50,000 in your area, and that the cost of building a new house is about £60 per square foot. A possible model, where y is the house price and x is the size of the house, would be:

$$y = 50,000 \div 60x$$

So if your house has 1,800 square feet, you could calculate that:

$$y = 50,000 + (60 \times 1,800) = 158,000$$

According to the model, you should get £158,000 for the house. If you knew, though, that houses of similar size in your area actually sell for from anything between £70,000 and £250,000, you wouldn't have achieved much.

A more realistic probabilistic model where ε represents the difference between the estimated price and the actual selling price, would be:

$$y = 50,000 + 60x + \varepsilon$$

where ε is a random quantity. This is called a simple linear regression model. The general formula for it is:

$$y = a + bx + \varepsilon$$

where a is the point where the line crosses the y axis, b is the slope of the line, y is the dependent variable, x is the independent variable and ε is the random error.

You might, for example, suppose that ε was a normal variable with a mean of 0. In this case, the average price for a house with a floor area of x would be 50,000 + 60x, but the actual prices would be normally distributed around this value. You would need to look carefully at any data you had available to test the effectiveness of your model. If it seemed to fit your data, you could use it to predict the range of prices that your house might fetch.

Determining a linear model from data: least squares analysis

In the example above, we tried to propose a linear model for house prices based on some external data we had available (the cost of the land and of building). However, if we have a large amount of house price/size data available already (and/or if we don't really believe that houses prices are simply related to building costs) it may be better to just take this data and try to find the linear relationship which fits the data best, without trying to explain how this relationship comes about. The method of least squares does precisely this. Consider the following six observations of x and y:

x	3	6	12	15	18	22
y	100	80	60	50	15	6

You can plot these points on a graph to get a scattergram as in Figure 4.6. The scattergram tells you that there is almost a linear relationship, so we can apply a linear model. The points aren't in a perfectly straight line, but we would like to draw the line that best fits the observations so that we can estimate future observations along the line as accurately as possible. This is done by working out a line that minimises the sum of the squared differences between the line and the observations, and is called the 'least squares method'. The line it produces is called the 'regression line'.

The formulae for calculating this line can be written in various equivalent ways. One way is to calculate:

1   The mean of x values is $\bar{x} = \Sigma x \div n$
2   The mean of y values is $\bar{y} = \Sigma y \div n$
3   The sum of the squares of the x values is Σx^2
4   The sum of the squares of the y values is Σy^2
5   The sum of the products of the x and y values is Σxy

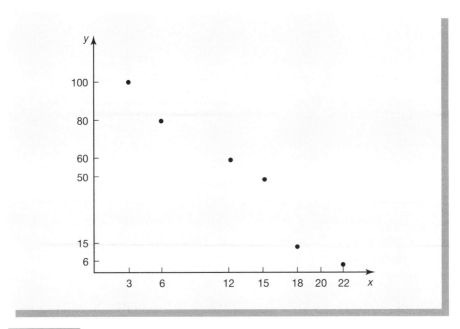

Figure 4.6   Scattergram of six observations

Here n is the number of data points and Σ means add up the value of the given variables for each data point.

In our example we obtain:

$$\bar{x} = 76 \div 6 = 12.67$$
$$\bar{y} = 311 \div 6 = 51.83$$
$$\Sigma x^2 = 9 + 36 + 144 + 225 + 324 + 484 = 1{,}222$$
$$\Sigma y^2 = 10{,}000 + 6{,}400 + 3{,}600 + 2{,}500 + 225 + 36 = 22{,}761$$
$$\Sigma xy = 300 + 480 + 720 + 750 + 270 + 132 = 2{,}652$$

Next, we calculate certain quantities that are conventionally called Sxy, Sxx, and Syy that are related to the variance and covariance of the x and y values:

$$Sxx = \Sigma x^2 - n\bar{x}^2$$
$$Syy = \Sigma y^2 - n\bar{y}^2$$
$$Sxy = \Sigma x - n\bar{x}\bar{y}$$

Incidentally, the correlation coefficient r is:

$$r = Sxy \div \sqrt{(Sxx \times Syy)}$$

In our example this gives:

$$Sxx = 1,222 - (6 \times 12.67^2) = 1,222 - 963.17 = 258.83$$
$$Syy = 22,761 - (6 \times 51.83^2) = 22,761 - 16,118.09 = 6,642.91$$
$$Sxy = 2,652 - (6 \times 12.67 \times 51.83) = 2,652 - 3,940.12 = -1,288.12$$

Finally, the formulae for the line $y = a + bx$ which best fits the data is given by:

$$b = Sxy \div Sxx$$
$$a = y - bx$$

So the line is:

$$y = 114.93 - 4.98x$$

which is the line plotted in Figure 4.7. It is interesting that the formulae for a and b always ensure that the line passes through the point $\bar{x}, \bar{y}$ given by the means of the x and y values.

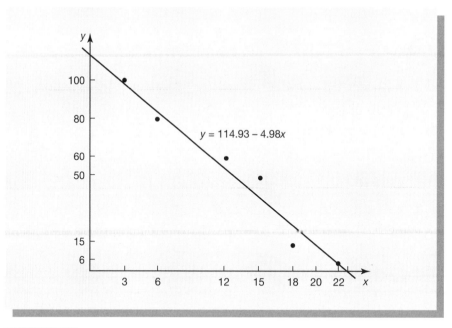

Figure 4.7   Line obtained by the least squares method

The sum of squares for error

We can measure how well the line $y = 114.93 - 4.98x$ fits the observed data by working out the differences between the points in the scattergram and the line. These differences are the observed values of the error variable a, and are called the 'residuals'.

The regression technique has found the line that fits the data best, in the sense that the sum of squared errors (in other words, the squares of each residual added together) will be the smallest possible for any straight line. There are a large number of tests you can do with the residuals to find out more about regression lines.

A new development: Reference Class Forecasting

In 2002 a Princeton psychology professor, Daniel Kahnemann, was awarded a Nobel Prize in economics for his work on Prospect Theory, an approach to explaining how people fail to evaluate risks and rewards accurately in many circumstances. Reference Class Forecasting was developed from Prospect Theory by Bent Flyvberg, an expert on the planning of 'mega-projects', which are mostly very large construction projects such as the Burj Khalifa tower in Dubai, the Channel Tunnel and the new Hong Kong airport, but also include aircraft programmes such as Concorde.

Flyvberg has shown in a study of 258 megaprojects all over the world over a 70-year period that almost 90% of these projects underestimated their eventual cost, by an average of 28%. Rail projects were the worst culprits, underestimating costs by 45% on average. Over the 70-year period he examined, Flyvberg did not find evidence that people had got any better at estimating costs, in spite of the use of increasingly sophisticated planning methods, and although projects in the developing world tended to underestimate by a higher margin, the problem of serious underestimation was broadly distributed geographically. This study was completed some years before the advent of Prospect Theory, and Flyvberg confined his explanations of why these underestimates might occur, along with the many serious errors in assessing the economic viability of projects and their social and environmental impact, to a discussion of factors such as a lack of transparency in the planning process and the potential incentives for participants to underestimate. For example, a contractor might knowingly underestimate the time and materials required for a specific task in order to win a bidding competition, and politicians might deliberately misrepresent the costs of a project in order to push it through and thereby benefit their own political careers.

Prospect Theory, however, looks not at deliberate miscalculation, which Flyvberg calls 'strategic misrepresentation', but at how people are psychologically prone to make mistakes in assessing risks (which Kahnemann explains as an 'optimism bias'). According to Flyvberg, combining these two types of explanation makes sense because optimism bias is strong in situations where incentives for strategic misrepresentation are low, and vice versa. Part of Kahnemann and his colleague Amos Tversky's work was to show that both amateurs and experts make similar mistakes in estimating, and have a systematic and predictable tendency to:

- underestimate costs, completion times and the risks of specific actions;
- overestimate benefits;
- see their project as unique.

In other words, people tend to have a bias towards optimism that is predictable and measurable. Flyvberg then made the rather obvious suggestion that if you force all megaproject planners to go through a systematic process of comparing their forecasts with the actual results of other megaprojects that have been completed, it might be possible to adjust for this optimism bias and obtain more accurate estimates.

This is what Reference Class Forecasting is all about. By collecting a 'reference class' (i.e. a group) of similar completed projects that is sufficiently large to be statistically significant, the Reference Class approach aims to compare the estimates of the new project with the outcomes of earlier ones. The aim is to 'regress' the new project's forecasts towards the average outcomes in the reference class.

The first practical use of Reference Class Forecasting was in 2004, when the UK's Department of Transport (DoT) introduced it in order to address the problem of cost and schedule overruns on large transportation projects. The DoT argued that in the past, the political-institutional 'climate' had been such that very few participants had had any incentive to avoid optimism bias. In the case of urban rail projects, for example, the DoT said that cities compete aggressively to gain government funding for their own projects, and thus have an incentive to present their plans in the best possible light.

Owing to the length of the projects, it is still too early to judge the success of Reference Class Forecasting in practice, but a number of other countries, such as The Netherlands and Switzerland, have adopted the method, and the American Planning Association has supported its introduction.

Summary

As we have seen, the main problem of forecasting is nothing to do with the various methods you can use to make an estimate about the future. The real problem is getting the message across about what the estimate really represents, in the sense of how it has been calculated and what assumptions have been made. Once a forecast is 'out there' and is made available to others, it often takes on a life of its own, and much of its value is lost. On the whole, professional forecasters do understand the limitations of forecasts perfectly well; it's the decision-making processes in large organisations that often fail to deal with forecasts sensibly, as is clearly demonstrated by the poor forecasting record of megaprojects around the world.

5

Key decision-making tools

This chapter introduces a number of powerful tools for analysing frequently occurring business problems:

- Game theory, which deals with problems of getting the best result when you are opposed by someone who is able as you are.
- Markov chains, which describe how some situations tend to stabilise over time.
- Network analysis, which is a useful technique for controlling a complex project.
- Queuing, which is a way of working out how long an 'arrival' will have to wait before being dealt with.

Game theory

Game theory was invented to try to explain business situations where the key players have opposing motives. The word 'game' is used to mean the conflict between these players; the players could be individuals, small companies, vast corporations, political parties, governments or even forces of nature. Deciding where to site a shop, planning an advertising campaign and deciding on an election strategy are all activities that can be examined by game theory.

Suppose you have two directly competing companies in a marketplace, Shoe World and Shoeland, both of which sell shoes. The week before the start of the school year is coming up, and both companies usually offer 10% or 20% discounts on their products. If they both give the same discount, they both know that Shoe World will get 70% of the total sales. If

Shoe World gives the bigger discount, they both know that Shoe World will get 85% of the total sales, and if Shoeland gives a bigger discount than Shoe World, they both know that Shoeland will get 60% of the total sales.

Suppose that both companies know all about each other, and all about the marketplace. What strategies can they each adopt to get the best share? We will assume that for this particular week the companies are only concerned with maximising their market share; for this promotion they are not concerned with maximising their profit, which would depend on their discount as well as their market share.

Table 5.1 shows the possible shares Shoe World can get depending on the discounts.

Table 5.1 Possible market shares for Shoe World

		Shoeland	
		10% discount	20% discount
Shoe World	10% discount	70% share	40% share
	20% discount	85% share	70% share

What should Shoe World do? If it offers a 10% discount, then Shoeland could give a 20% discount, and Shoe World would only get 40% of the sales. If it offers a 20% discount, Shoeland could also give a 20% discount, and Shoe World will get 70% of the sales. Shoe World decides to give a 20% discount.

Shoeland also considers what to do. If it offers a 10% discount, Shoe World could give a 20% discount, and Shoeland would only get 15% (100% – 85%) of the sales. If it offers a 20% discount, Shoe World could give a 20% discount, and Shoeland would get 30% (100% – 70%) of the sales. Shoeland decides to give a 20% discount.

Both companies have tried to protect themselves, and both have decided to give a 20% discount, so Shoe World will get 70% of the sales and Shoeland will get 30%. This kind of game is called a 'zero-sum' game, meaning that any gain that one side makes will be at the expense of the other. Notice that the outcome has been to offer heavier discounts, presumably reducing profit margins for both companies.

The table we used to work out the possible shares is called a 'pay-off matrix'. One player is called the 'row player', and the other is called the 'column player'. The row player's choices (which can be written as RI, R2 ... Rm) are listed down the left-hand side of the matrix and the column player's choices (which can be written as (Cl, C2 ... Cm) are listed along the top.

The convention is to write the pay-off to the row player in the matrix for each combination of row and column player moves. In this case the column player's possible outcomes are obtained by subtracting the row player's pay-off from 100. The row player wants to maximise the outcomes in the matrix, and the column player wants to minimise the outcomes, so they can be called the 'maximising player' and the 'minimising player' respectively.

Example

Mark and Sally are competing ice-cream sellers with two possible spots to sell from, a school or a park. There is a total of £6,000 that can be made, and if they go to different places, they'll make £3,000 each. If they both go to the school, Mark will only make £2,500, and if they both go to the park, he will make £3,500. Where should they go?

Making Mark the row player, we can write the matrix as shown in Table 5.2.

Table 5.2 Competing to sell ice cream

		Sally	
		School	Park
Mark	School	2,500	3,000
	Park	3,000	3,500

Mark works out that if he goes to the park, the least he will make is £3,000, so he goes there. Sally works out that if she goes to the school the least she can make is £3,000, so she goes there, and they both make £3,000. Their choices are called the 'optimal' solutions, which means the best they can do by playing safe.

Strictly determined games

The two games we have looked at are called 'strictly determined games'. To test whether a game is strictly determined, the steps are:

Step 1. Find the smallest number in each row and write it at the end of the row.

Step 2. Pick the biggest of these numbers – this may be the optimal solution for the row player.

Step 3. Find the largest number in each column and write it underneath the column.

Step 4. Pick the smallest of these numbers – this may be the optimal solution for the column player.

Step 5. Is the number you got in step 2 equal to the number you got in step 4? If so, the game is strictly determined. If it isn't strictly determined, you must use different methods which we'll examine later.

In strictly determined games, the optimal solutions give the same number, which is called the 'saddle point'.

Example

Two major banks are competing to attract young people to open accounts with them, knowing that once they have opened an account they will probably stay with the bank for life. It is therefore worth offering a fairly substantial free gift. Bank A is trying to decide between offering book tokens, clothes vouchers or a computer. Bank B is trying to decide between a TV, a computer game or a voucher for sports goods. Both banks have access to the same market research, which shows the possible shares of the estimated 240,000 customers this scheme will attract. The matrix, with Bank A as the row player, looks like Table 5.3.

Table 5.3 Free gifts from banks to win customers

		Bank B		
		Game	*TV*	*Sports*
	Book	10	14	18
Bank A	*Clothes*	12	16	14
	Computer	10	12	8

In Table 5.3, the numbers in the matrix give the number (in tens of thousands) of customers.

First, let's test to see if this is a strictly determined game (Table 5.4); find the smallest number in each row and the biggest in each column that Bank A will attract for each of the combinations of Bank A and Bank B's incentives.

Table 5.4 Finding the minima and maxima

		Bank B			
		Game	TV	Sports	Row minima
Bank A	Book	10	14	18	10
	Clothes	12	16	14	12
	Computer	10	12	8	8
	Column maxima	12	16	18	

The biggest of the smallest row numbers (the row minima) is 12, and the smallest of the biggest column numbers is 12, so the game is strictly determined and the optimal solution is for Bank A to offer a clothes voucher, and for Bank B to offer a computer game – that way, they will carve up the market equally with 120,000 customers each.

Real-life stories   **Game theory in real life: voting systems**

Political scientists have gained many useful insights by applying game theory to voting systems. One of the best known is 'Duverger's Law', which states that 'single-member district plurality' voting systems (SMDPs) tends to create two-party political systems. SMDPs are voting systems where each voter has one vote which they can cast for one candidate in their district, and only one candidate can win the district. The UK and Canada, for example, have SMDP systems.

One of the features of SMDPs is that a minority party that always comes second or third in every district will end up with no winning candidates, so any minority party that has a wide geographical distribution is likely to be under-represented politically, considering the number of votes they actually receive overall. Knowing this, voters may not bother to vote for minority parties on the grounds that they never seem to win. On the other hand, if supporters of a minority party are concentrated as a majority in a few districts, the party will win those districts, and there will be more than two parties in the political system.

Duverger's Law should not really be seen as a law, but as a tendency. Maurice Duverger, its discoverer, argued that SMDPs simply tended to delay the rise of a new political party, and speed up the collapse of a declining party.

Strategies

In real life, strictly determined games do occur, but more often games are not strictly determined; that is, that they do not have a saddle point. This means that the players must vary their moves to keep their opponents off balance: they must have a so-called 'mixed strategy'.

Consider a game where two players show the side of a coin. If both coins show heads or both show tails, one player wins £1 (let's call this player 'Same') and if one coin shows heads and the other one shows tails, the other player wins £1 (let's call this player 'Different').

Making Same the row player, the matrix is given in Table 5.5.

Table 5.5 Coin-flipping game

		Different	
		H	T
Same	H	1	−1
	T	−1	1

In this type of game, this is called the pay-off matrix. If one of the players always shows the same side of the coin, the other one can spot the strategy and counter it, winning all the time. Suppose, instead, that Same decides to show heads at random 1 time in 4, and Different decides to show the heads at random 1 time in 6. The frequency of the possible combinations would look like this:

Heads, heads $\frac{1}{4} \times \frac{1}{6} = \frac{1}{24}$

Tails, tails $\frac{3}{4} \times \frac{5}{6} = \frac{15}{24}$

Heads, tails $\frac{1}{4} \times \frac{5}{6} = \frac{5}{24}$

Tails, heads $\frac{3}{4} \times \frac{1}{6} = \frac{3}{24}$

Same would win 1/24 + 15/24 = 16/24ths of the time, and lose 5/24 + 3/24 = 8/24ths of the time. On average, Same would win a total of 16/24 – 8/24 = 8/24 per game, or £8 every 24 plays.

Having played a losing game for a while, Different decides to reverse his strategy by showing heads 5 times in 6. The frequency of the possible combinations now looks like this:

Heads, heads $\frac{1}{4} \times \frac{5}{6} = \frac{5}{24}$

Tails, tails $\frac{3}{4} \times \frac{1}{6} = \frac{3}{24}$

Heads, tails $\frac{1}{4} \times \frac{1}{6} = \frac{1}{24}$

Tails, heads $\frac{3}{4} \times \frac{5}{6} = \frac{15}{24}$

Same now wins 5/24 + 3/24 = 8/24ths of the time and loses 1/24 +15/24 = 16/24. So now, on average, Same loses 8/24 – 16/24 = – 8/24, or £8 pounds to Different every 24 plays.

In fact, there is a best strategy for this game, which is to show either heads or tails with probability 1/2. Suppose that Same adopts this strategy but Different shows heads with probability p, and tails with probability 1 – p. Same will win $1/2p + \frac{1}{2}(1 - p) = \frac{1}{2}$ of the time. On average, neither player wins whatever value of p Different chooses.

If Same chooses any other strategy, Different can choose a value of p which will ensure that in the long run Different will win. So Same should choose the ½, ½ strategy. Similarly, Different will choose ½, ½ or else Same will win in the long run. The solution of the game is therefore for both players to play the same ½, ½ strategy.

Dominance

If you have a game in which there are two rows, a and b, in which the numbers in row b are all less than or equal to the numbers in the same position in row a, row b is 'dominated' by row a. The row player never needs to play a move from row b because he can always do as well, if not better, by making a move from row a. The same works for columns and the column player. Dominance enables us to remove the dominated rows and columns from a game to make it easier to deal with.

Example

Suppose you have the game:

```
  2    -1
 -3     1
  1    -0
```

You can simplify this game to a 2 × 2 form because the row [2 –1] dominates the row [1 –3].

Taking out the row [1 –3] gives you:

```
  2    -1
 -3     1
```

Test yourself: Part 7

In the children's game 'Rock, Scissors, Paper', two opponents choose one of the three items simultaneously. Rock beats scissors, scissors beats paper, and paper beats rock. Answer the following questions:

1   Is there a winning strategy for this game?

2   Is there a losing strategy?

3   Is this a zero-sum game?

See page 203 for the answers.

Game theory summary

Game theory problems often appear in business situations that are particularly tough, such as in markets that have become commoditised; if all the competitors are selling the same products – or products that are perceived as very similar by customers – then the competition revolves around the price, and profit margins are driven down. This is why businesses make such great efforts to develop products and services that are differentiated from their competitors', and to build brands that make them appear special. When faced with game-like situations against well-matched opponents, most businesses would rather tip over the board and change the rules in their favour. Nevertheless, processes such as auctions, competitive bids, supply chains and competition for market share can all be analysed usefully using game theory. It is also a useful tool when considering long-term strategic issues; although it often won't provide a precise answer, it can improve managers' grasp of the dynamics of business interactions and help them to make better decisions.

Markov chains

Events that happen in stages can frequently be represented by 'Markov chains', allowing future events to be estimated. Markov chains were originally developed by Andrei Markov for the study of the motion of particles in gases, but have since been applied with great success to business. They can be used, for example, to estimate the loyalty of purchasers to brand names, future bad debts, and the movement of purchasers between competing companies.

Markov chains are calculated using matrices, so we should remind ourselves of how matrices work.

Matrices and vectors

Matrices are rectangular arrays of numbers. This is a matrix:

$$
\begin{matrix}
4 & 3 & 2 \\
5 & 7 & 2
\end{matrix}
$$

The position of each number is important in a matrix. A matrix is only equal to another matrix if the numbers are the same and in the same places. However, we could turn the rows into columns and the columns into rows in the matrix above and get:

$$
\begin{matrix}
4 & 5 \\
3 & 7 \\
2 & 2
\end{matrix}
$$

which is called the 'transpose' of the first matrix.

To add matrices together, you add the numbers in the corresponding positions. To add the matrices:

$$
A = \begin{matrix} 2 & 4 \\ 6 & 8 \end{matrix} \quad \text{and} \quad B = \begin{matrix} 1 & 3 \\ 5 & 7 \end{matrix}
$$

you add the number in each place to the number in the same place in the other matrix:

$$
A + B = \begin{matrix} 2+1 & 4+3 \\ 6+5 & 8+7 \end{matrix} = \begin{matrix} 3 & 7 \\ 11 & 15 \end{matrix}
$$

To multiply a matrix by a number, you simply multiply each of the numbers in the matrix by the number; $2 \times$ Matrix A is:

$$
2A = \begin{matrix} 4 & 8 \\ 12 & 16 \end{matrix}
$$

To multiply a matrix by another matrix, you multiply the rows of the first matrix by the columns of the second matrix. For example, to multiply Matrix A by Matrix B:

$$
AB = \begin{matrix} 2 & 4 \\ 6 & 8 \end{matrix} \times \begin{matrix} 1 & 3 \\ 5 & 7 \end{matrix}
$$

we proceed as follows. To compute the number in the first row and column of AB, take the first row of A, (2 4), multiply each number by the number in the corresponding position in the first column of B, (1 5) and add the results together:

$$
(2 \times 1) + (4 \times 5) = 22
$$

To find the number in the first row and second column of AB, multiply the numbers in the first row of A by the numbers in the second column of B, and add them together:

$$(2 \times 3) + (4 \times 7) = 6 + 28 = 34$$

Repeat the process for the other row and column, and matrix AB will look like this:

AB =	$(2 \times 1) + (4 \times 5)$	$(2 \times 3) + (4 \times 7)$
	$(6 \times 1) + (8 \times 5)$	$(6 \times 3) + (8 \times 7)$

AB =	22	34
	46	74

Now for one of the differences between ordinary multiplication and matrix multiplication; with matrices, A × B does NOT always equal B × A. Multiplying B × A, we get:

BA =	1	3	×	2	4
	5	7		6	8
=	$(1 \times 2) + (3 \times 6)$			$(1 \times 4) + (3 \times 8)$	
	$(5 \times 2) + (7 \times 6)$			$(5 \times 4) + (7 \times 8)$	
=	21	28			
	52	76			

You may occasionally find that AB does equal BA, but most often it doesn't.

A *vector* is just a matrix consisting of a single column, such as:

4
3

We will need to multiply vectors by matrices, and this is done in the same way as the multiplication of matrices, except that the top number of the vector is used for the first column of the matrix, and the bottom number of the vector is used for the second column of the matrix. Since the vector only has one column, the answer will also only have one column and thus will be another vector. For example,

1	2	×	4	=	$(1 \times 4) + (2 \times 3)$	=	10
4	7		3		$(4 \times 4) + (7 \times 3)$		37

There is much more to know about matrices and vectors, but this is enough for us to look at the principles of Markov chains.

The regular Markov chain

Suppose there are only two beer producers in a particular market: a large company, which brews the brand Jupiter beer, and a smaller company, which is gaining in the marketplace with its brand Odin beer. Market research is done to find out the companies' respective market shares and also the tendency for drinkers to switch brands. What can be forecast for future years?

Jupiter beer has an 80% share of the market, so Odin beer has a 20% share. Due to management policies and other factors, every year Jupiter loses 4/7ths of its customers to Odin, and Odin loses 2/3rds of its customers to Jupiter. What share will the companies each have after one year?

After one year, Jupiter will have kept 3/7ths of its own market share, and gained 2/3rds of Odin's, so it will have 3/7 + 2/3, and Odin will have kept 1/3 of its own share and gained 4/7ths of Jupiter's share. Calling Jupiter's original share J0 and its share after 1 year J1, and Odin's original share O0 and its share after 1 year O1, the calculation can be written as:

$$\begin{pmatrix} J1 \\ O1 \end{pmatrix} = \begin{pmatrix} \frac{3}{7} & \frac{2}{3} \\ \frac{4}{7} & \frac{1}{3} \end{pmatrix} \times \begin{pmatrix} J0 \\ O0 \end{pmatrix}$$

This is a matrix calculation. Proceeding as in the previous section, we multiply the top row by the vector [J0 O0], which is $\left[\frac{8}{10} \frac{2}{10} \right]$ and get:

$$J1 = \left(\frac{3}{7} \times \frac{8}{10} \right) + \left(\frac{2}{3} \times \frac{2}{10} \right)$$

$$= \frac{10}{21}$$

Multiplying the bottom row by [J0 O0] we get:

$$O1 = \left(\frac{4}{7} \times \frac{8}{10} \right) + \left(\frac{1}{3} \times \frac{2}{10} \right)$$

$$= \frac{11}{21}$$

The numbers J1 and O1 are the proportions that the two companies respectively hold of the market $\left[\frac{10}{21} \frac{11}{21} \right]$ after one year. Notice that their proportions must add up to 1 (e.g. 100% of the market). After one year Jupiter has lost a large share of the market to Odin.

Suppose that the factors influencing the movement of customers between the two beer companies do not change in future years. What will their market shares be after the second and third years?

To find the answer after the second year, we call their shares at the end of the second year J2 and O2 respectively. [J2 O2] is found by multiplying the original matrix by [J1 O1]:

$$\begin{pmatrix} J2 \\ O2 \end{pmatrix} = \begin{pmatrix} \frac{3}{7} & \frac{2}{3} \\ \frac{4}{7} & \frac{1}{3} \end{pmatrix} \times \begin{pmatrix} J1 \\ O1 \end{pmatrix}$$

[J1 O1] is [10/21 11/21], so:

$$J2 = \left(\frac{3}{7} \times \frac{10}{21} \right) + \left(\frac{2}{3} \times \frac{11}{21} \right)$$
$$= 0.5533$$

Expressing J2 as a fraction is a bit awkward, so we can give it as 0.5533 correct to four decimal places. To obtain O2:

$$O2 = \left(\frac{4}{7} \times \frac{10}{21} \right) + \left(\frac{1}{3} \times \frac{11}{21} \right)$$
$$= 0.4467$$

The market shares [J2 O2] aren't very different from [J1 O1]: very roughly, they are still hovering around the halfway mark. Now to find out what happens after the third year:

$$\begin{pmatrix} J3 \\ O3 \end{pmatrix} = \begin{pmatrix} \frac{3}{7} & \frac{2}{3} \\ \frac{4}{7} & \frac{1}{3} \end{pmatrix} \times \begin{pmatrix} J2 \\ O2 \end{pmatrix}$$

Calculate J3:

$$J3 = \left(\frac{3}{7} \times 0.5533 \right) + \left(\frac{2}{3} \times 0.4467 \right)$$
$$= 0.2371 + 0.2978$$
$$= 0.5349$$

Calculate O3:

$$O3 = \left(\frac{4}{7} \times 0.5533 \right) + \left(\frac{1}{3} \times 0.4467 \right)$$
$$= 0.3162 + 0.1489$$
$$= 0.4651$$

The difference between [J3 O3], which is [0.5349 0.4651] and [J2 O2], which is [0.5533 0.4467] is smaller than the difference between [J2 O2] and [J1 O1].

This is one of the discoveries of the Markov chain: that over time, the situation stabilises. In our example, after the initial setback, Jupiter will continue to enjoy a roughly 50/50 split of the market with Odin in the future.

Note, however, that we have assumed that the factors causing the brand switching between Jupiter and Odin will remain constant. In real life, the beer companies may change their policies, and customers may change their behaviour, so the Markov chain calculation may not produce a very accurate forecast; what it does do, however, is show us what will happen if nothing changes, which may help us to decide how we should change our sales approach.

Probabilistic interpretations of Markov chains

Our calculation above uses a deterministic interpretation of the Markov chain; the proportion of customers changing allegiance each year is given as a definite fraction. It is more usual to think of Markov chains in terms of probabilities. In this case we should think of a single beer drinker who can be in one of two states: preferring Jupiter or preferring Odin. The Markov matrix then gives the probabilities of the beer drinker changing preferences each year. Since Jupiter loses 4/7ths of its customers each year, we deduce that if the beer drinker prefers Jupiter beer one year, the probability that the beer drinker will prefer Odin beer the next year is 4 in 7, so the probability that the beer drinker will prefer Jupiter beer in the second year is only 3 in 7. Similarly, if the beer drinker prefers Odin in the first year, the probability of preferring it in the second is 1 in 3 and the probability of changing preference is 2 in 3. These are the same numbers as we had before.

In this version of the Markov chain our earlier calculations have the following interpretation:

> *regardless of the beer drinker's initial state, in the long term the probability of the drinker being in each of the two possible states is roughly 50/50.*

The probabilistic interpretation explains various terms used in conjunction with Markov chains. Each row and column of the Markov matrix corresponds to a particular 'state' (preferring Jupiter is one state and preferring Odin is another). If you have an entry in, say, column 'i' and row 'j', the entry gives you the probability of moving from state 'i' to state 'j' in one time step; this is called a 'transition probability', and the whole matrix is called a 'transition matrix'. Note that the columns always add up to 1, and that all the entries are positive; such a matrix is called a 'stochastic matrix'.

Absorbing Markov chains

Some probabilistic Markov chains are called 'absorbing'. Absorbing Markov chains deal with random processes which sometimes enter an 'absorbing' state from which they can never leave. An interesting business application for this is in credit control, when account managers are interested in finding the probability or a debt becoming a bad debt (an absorbing state) or being paid (another absorbing state) and how long this will probably take.

Markov chains in real life

Markov chains are applied quite widely to business problems, most notably in modelling credit control risks, market behaviour and customer relationships. For example, mail-order catalogue firms often model the probable behaviour of their customers over time, using Markov chains to decide when to stop sending marketing material to a customer, when is the best time to send them a new offer, and so on, depending on when customers have made a purchase.

Markov chains are being used extensively by internet businesses. Google's system of assigning a 'PageRank' to webpages as a way of measuring the relative importance of each webpage depended on a Markov Chain. Google has now removed PageRank from its array of webmaster tools, apparently because it felt that website owners were becoming over-reliant on it as a single measure of the popularity of their webpages. Other internet firms are using Markov Chains to try to model how internet users navigate the web.

Controlling a project with network analysis

A team of people works on a project. They all know that the project must have an overall plan and that managers must coordinate the plan, but is this happening in practice? As projects become increasingly complex, systematic planning becomes the only way to keep control of them. The kind of planning necessary to put people on the moon or build a high-tech weapon has a wide variety of applications in more mundane businesses; it is called 'network analysis'.

To take a simple example, suppose it is your responsibility to organise a day's seminar. You must find the venue, design a programme, send the invitations, organise the catering, make sure there are enough chairs, arrange for the audio-visual equipment, check that the speakers are briefed, and so on. Some tasks will have to be done before the others, and most must be completed before the seminar can start. You have a budget to keep within, but you have the power to decide how much will be spent on what; if the catering turns out to be more expensive than anticipated, you will have to spend less money on other things. You could run the whole thing by the seat of your pants, but it is more sensible to plan out all the tasks in an ordered, rational way, which can be done by drawing a network to represent the various tasks. To draw the network, you have to list all the activities and then work out their precedence in a table. This is almost always a team activity, since it requires everyone who has special knowledge to give their opinion on what can be done before what and how long it will take. Giving a letter of the alphabet to each task or activity, a precedence table might look like the one in Table 5.6.

Table 5.6 Precedence table

Task	Preceding activity
B,C	A
D, E, F	C
G	B, D, E
H, I	F
J	H
K	J, I, G

This can be drawn as a diagram, as in Figure 5.1.

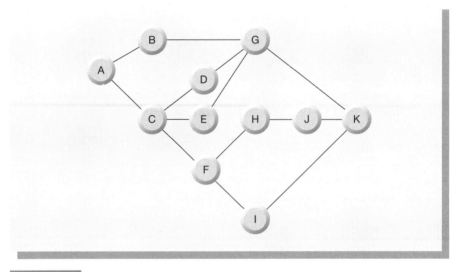

Figure 5.1   A network of tasks

Working out the precedence table is often the hardest part of making the analysis. Figure 5.1 shows the network of different tasks that will result from the precedence table in Table 5.6. Drawing networks, especially com-plicated ones, usually takes more than one attempt. Try breaking down the network into 'subnetworks'; for instance, you could draw the first three rows of the precedence table in Table 5.6 as three different subnet-works, as in Figure 5.2.

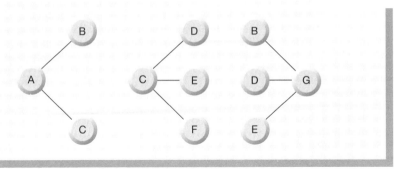

Figure 5.2   Subnetworks

Once you have drawn all the subnetworks, you can check that they are correct, and then work out how they all connect up together, making sure that you have not created a circle of precedence (for instance 'A precedes B precedes C precedes A').

In Figures 5.1 and 5.2 the points where lines meet are called 'nodes'. Each node has a letter which refers to a completed activity. Another way of noting the activities is to write the letters against the line that represents the activity and to give each node a number, as in Figure 5.3.

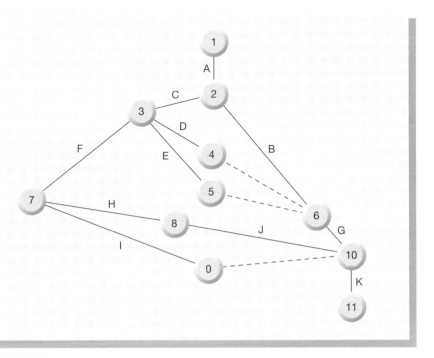

Figure 5.3   Node network

This method enables you to describe each activity by the numbers in the nodes at the ends of the corresponding line. It is preferable to avoid having two or more activities with the same end nodes, so you introduce new end nodes and join the end nodes by a dotted line; the dotted lines are called 'dummy activities' because they are simply there to make the system work. In Figure 5.3, D and F both start from node 3; so that they don't both end on node 6, a dummy is inserted.

Suppose you have the following estimates for how many hours each task or activity will take:

A	B	C	D	E	F	G	H	I
2	3	4	5	3	2	6	3	2

As we already know, some of the activities can take place at the same time as others. To find out how long the whole project will take to complete, you have to find the longest path through the network, which is known as the 'critical path'. Listing each route along the network, we get:

Route	Time	
A B G K	2 + 3 + 6 + 4	= 15
A C D Dummy G K	2 + 4 + 5 + 6 + 4	= 21
A C E Dummy G K	2 + 4 + 3 + 6 + 4	= 19
A C F H J K	2 + 4 + 2 + 3 + 2 + 4	= 17
A C F I Dummy K	2 + 4 + 2 + 2 + 4	= 14

The critical path is A C D Dummy G K, which will take 21 hours. This would be very hard to work out if you just had the precedence table but no network.

When networks are very large, it is quite easy to miss some of the paths. This can be avoided by marking the 'earliest event times'. This is done by dividing the circle of each node and then dividing the right-hand half again. The left-hand side of the circle has the node's number, and the top right-hand quarter has the time elapsed from the start along the longest path to that point. Figure 5.4 shows how this is done.

In Figure 5.4, the earliest event time at node 3 is 6, because A takes 2 hours and C takes 4 hours, and 2 + 4 = 6. The earliest event time at node 6 is the time it takes along the longest route to get there, which is A C D Dummy, or 2 + 4 + 5 = 11. You don't need to start at the beginning to calculate the earliest event time at each node. Calculate the earliest event times in order of precedence. Once the earliest event times for all the nodes preceding the one of interest have been calculated you can find its earliest

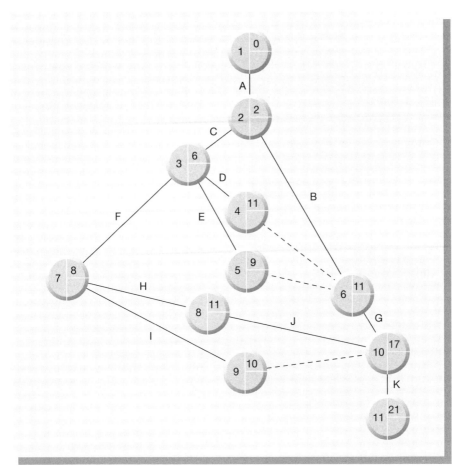

Figure 5.4   Earliest event times

event time thus: for each immediately preceding node, take its earliest event time plus the activity time joining the two nodes, and then take the maximum of these over all the preceding nodes. For example, having calculated that the earliest event time at node 6 is 11, at node 8 is 11 and at node 9 is 10, we find that the earliest event time at node 10 is the maximum of 11 + 6, 11 + 2, and 10 + 0 (dummy activities take no time), so the earliest event time at node 10 is 17. This process will give you the time for the critical path at the final node. However, it doesn't tell you which is the critical path, so we use the remaining space in each circle to write the 'latest event time'. At the final node, the latest event time is the same as the earliest event time 21. To find the latest event times at the other nodes, you simply work backwards along the paths, subtracting the time

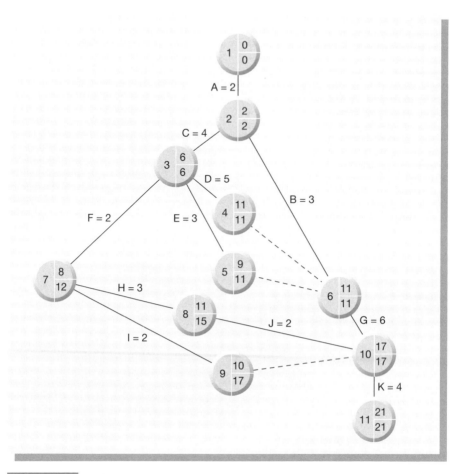

Figure 5.5   Completed node network

of the task you are moving past from the total and choosing the minimum of these numbers when a node is connected to more than one later node; thus, the latest event time at node 10 is 21 — K, which is 17. Figure 5.5 shows the completed network.

The critical path is the path where the earliest event times and the latest event times are equal at each node; sometimes you have more than one path meeting this condition, in which case all are critical

PERT

The Project Evaluation and Review Technique, or PERT, is used when you can't be sure that you have estimated the times of activities accurately. Suppose you are building a hotel in a developing country which is politically unstable; you might know how to keep everything to schedule back home, but out here there are many unfamiliar factors that can cause things to go wrong. With PERT, you make three different estimates for the length of time each activity will take. Calling the estimates a, b and c, a is the estimate where nothing goes wrong, and is the shortest of the three; b is the estimate of time where everything you can anticipate going wrong does so, and is the largest of the three estimates, and c is an estimate of the time it would take to complete an activity if it were repeated often, and is the middle estimate. The expected time of an activity can be found by weighting each of the variables. PERT suggests you use the formula:

$$\text{Expected time } (a + b + 4c) \div 6$$

For the following estimates of a project with three tasks, A, B and C, where each task must be completed before the next one commences:

Table 5.7 Estimates of a project with three tasks

Task	a	b	c
A	5 days	9 days	7 days
B	3 days	12 days	8 days
C	4 days	7 days	5 days

We can work out the expected times for A, B and C as:

$$A = (5 + 4 + 28) \div 6 = 6.16$$
$$B = (3 + 12 + 32) \div 6 = 7.83$$
$$C = (4 + 7 + 20) \div 6 = 5.16$$

Thus the total expected time for completion of the whole project is 6.16 + 7.83 + 5.16 = 19.15. Because we are working with estimates, we are likely to make errors in our predictions, so PERT estimates the standard deviation for each activity estimate as:

$$\text{Standard deviation for estimate} = (b - a) \div 6$$

The standard deviations for A, B and C are:

$$A = (9 - 5) \div 6 = 0.67$$
$$B = (12 - 3) \div 6 = 1.5$$
$$C = (7 - 4) \div 6 = 0.5$$

Adding the squares of the deviations we get:

$$0.67^2 + 1.5^2 + 0.5^2 = 0.45 + 2.25 + 0.25 = 2.95$$

Standard deviation for whole project = $\sqrt{2.95}$ = 1.72. Provided that there is a reasonably large number of tasks (perhaps 3 is not enough) it will be reasonable to assume that the total time is normally distributed, even though we have made a different assumption about the individual activity times.

Assuming that the total time of the activities is normally distributed, we can say with 95% confidence that the project will finish in less than:

$$\text{Expected time} + (1.645 \times \text{Standard deviation}) =$$
$$19.15 + (1.645 \times 1.72) = 19.15 + 2.8294$$
$$= 21.98$$

So we can say that we estimate that the project will take less than 22 days to finish.

Real-life stories   ### PERT in real life: Polaris

In the 1950s the US Navy was developing nuclear submarines, called Polaris, which could launch nuclear missiles. PERT was created as a way of controlling parts of the project, and received enthusiastic attention at the time as a cutting-edge management technique. During the 1960s PERT was quite widely adopted across many industries, and a whole industry of PERT trainers and consultants emerged. It remains a standard project management tool today.

PERT's main benefit is its method of network analysis, which in many cases can substantially reduce time and cost. Recently, however, attention has been drawn to PERT's limitations, such as that its elaborate charts can become very unwieldy, causing the technique to be abandoned during a project. According to critics, PERT was hyped by the US Navy as a stunning management innovation principally in order to fend off bureaucratic interference by the government, and was often only applied after the fact in reports to outsiders. More importantly, PERT has been found by many researchers to produce quite inaccurate estimates of how long it will take to complete a project. Although PERT is still being used, many project managers are turning to other techniques that may be better suited to their specific needs on a project.

Queueing

All of us have had some experience of the dynamics of waiting in queues; most of us have to cope with several queues every day: waiting in a car at a red light, buying stamps over the counter at a post office and so on. We feel strongly about queues. Some places seem to have their system well organised, so that people don't have to wait, while in others things seem to be poorly run. Our intuitive feeling that waiting time in queues could be lessened by good management is, of course, correct. There is a mathematics of queueing, and in this section we will look at its basics.

Queueing problems don't only occur on roads and in service settings. For example, loading and unloading a stream of lorries at a warehouse, maintaining a number of machines and processing work can all throw up queueing problems.

The input source

The input source is the population of potential customers (they needn't be human beings) who could enter the queue. The population can either be of finite size, or of effectively infinite size. If the rate at which new customers enter the queueing system is noticeably affected by the number of customers already in the queue, the input source is finite. For instance, if there are 20 waiters in a restaurant who must queue to collect meals from the kitchen, and 4 of them are queueing, there are only 16 other waiters in the population who could enter the queue, so the input source is finite.

An infinite input source refers to situations where the input source is so large that the number of customers in the queue has almost no effect on the rate at which new customers arrive. A bank has many thousands of customers, and only very few of them are at the bank at any one time, so the input source is said to be infinite.

Arrivals

The distribution of the probability of a certain number of customers arriving in a given amount of time is often described by the Poisson distribution. In this case, the formula for calculating the probability of n customers arriving in a given time period is·

$$P(A = n) = [(\lambda T)^n \div n!] \times e^{-\lambda T}$$

where A is the number of customers arriving during the time interval, T is the time period, λ is the mean number of customer arrivals per unit of time and e is the constant 2.7182818.

Example

Suppose that customers arrive at a shop counter at a rate of three per hour, so $\lambda = 3$. The probability that six customers will arrive in the next hour is:

$$N = 6 \qquad T = 1$$

$$\begin{aligned}
P(A = 6) &= [(3 \times 1)^6 \div 6!] \times e^{-3 \times 1} \\
&= [3^6 \div 720] \times e^{-3} \\
&= 1.01 e^{-3} \\
&= 0.05
\end{aligned}$$

If you wanted to work out the probable arrivals over 10 hours, T would be 10, and so on. Rates of arrival (λ) can be influenced by managers. For example, offering lower prices at certain times of the day, as telephone companies do, can reduce arrival rates at peak periods.

Balking and reneging

In queueing maths, 'patient' customers are those that enter a queue and stay in it until they are served. A driver in a traffic jam would be a patient customer because there is no escape from the queue. 'Impatient' customers are those who either see the size of the queue and decide not to enter it ('balking') or who enter a queue and then give up after waiting for a while ('reneging').

Single or multiple lines?

An organisation can usually choose whether to offer single or multiple service points. If you feel that customers want to be served in the order in which they arrive rather than on how well they guess which queue to join, you could provide a single service point, or multiple service points that had a single queue leading up to them. Multiple service points with multiple queues work well in places like supermarkets, where some of the service points are for 'baskets only' or some other limitation for customers who will spend less time making their purchases.

The distribution of service times

The probability that a customer will be served, after reaching the head of the queue, in no more than T time periods can often be described by an exponential distribution, using the formula:

$$PQ \ (t \text{ is less than or equal to } T) = 1 - e^{-\mu T}$$

where μ is the mean average of customers being served per unit of time t. The variance of the distribution of service time is $(1/\mu)^2$ and the mean is $1/\mu$.

Analysing rates of service

Suppose you manage a supermarket which provides a special counter for disabled people. You know that the disabled customers arrive at the counter at a mean rate of 25 an hour in a Poisson distribution, and that they are served at a mean rate of 30 customers an hour. You want to find the 'traffic density', or how much of the time your counter clerk is busy, the average number of customers in the queue, the average amount of time they spend waiting and being served and the average time they spend just waiting. To calculate these, we use the following formulae from queueing theory:

Traffic density (ρ) = λ/μ = 0.83, or 83%

Average number of customers in queue or being served

(L) = $\lambda \div (\mu - \lambda)$ = 25 ÷ (30 − 25) = 5

Average number of customers in the queue ρL= 0.83 × 5 = 4.15
Average time spent in the system (W) = 1 ÷ ($\mu - \lambda$) = 1 ÷ (30 − 25)
= 0.20%, or 12 minutes
Average time spent in the queue ρW = 0.83 × 0.2 = 0.17, or 10.28 minutes

Now you know a lot more about the experience your customer is having. Suppose that you now want to find what rate of service is necessary for customers to have to wait an average of only 6 minutes in the system; use the formula:

W = 1 ÷ ($\mu - \lambda$)

Substituting 6 minutes (0.10 of an hour) for W, we get:

0.1 = 1 ÷ (μ − 25)
0.1(μ − 25) = 1
0.1μ − 2.5 = 1
μ = 35

You would have to serve customers at a rate of 35 an hour.

More complex situations require more complex models which we won't go into here. One thing you should be aware of, though, is that many of these models assume a Poisson distribution for the arrivals and exponentially distributed service times. Often, the problems become so complex that this is no longer applicable; in these cases, computer simulation models are developed to estimate values and analyse the situation. Simulations have the advantage of being much less costly to experiment with than the real system, and they compress time; for example, you can simulate several years' worth of aeroplane arrivals and delays at an airport in a few minutes.

Real-life stories   Queueing theory in real life

Queueing occurs when the demand for a service or process exceeds the supply; this does not only apply to human queues, but to other systems such telecommunications traffic, transport systems, and manufacturing process. There is usually trade-off between eliminating queues altogether and allowing them to become very long. In many situations it is considered uneconomic to try to reduce waiting times to zero, because it would require keeping a lot of resources on standby just in case there was a sudden rush. In the aftermath of the 1989 San Francisco earthquake, for example, huge numbers of people tried to use the telephone, the system could not cope with the demand, and very few calls got through. It was argued later that it would not be economic to re-engineer the system to cope with a massive surge in demand, because even in San Francisco earthquakes occur quite rarely, and at unpredictable intervals.

Nevertheless, there are often situations where reducing queueing times can produce substantial savings. Recently, a Pennsylvania hospital, the Milton S. Hershey Medical Center, was faced with a surge in demand in its Emergency Department; the Emergency rooms were designed to cope with 30,000 patients a year, but demand had nearly doubled to 50,000 a year. Expanding the facilities to cope with the increased number of patients would have cost an estimated $20 million, so the hospital called in industrial engineers to examine whether they could improve waiting times in the existing facilities. The result was a technique called Physician Direction Queuing, which used queueing theory to speed up the process whereby the right medic saw the right patients. This required a much smaller expansion of the Emergency rooms than had originally been envisaged, saving $15 million, while dramatically reducing waiting times.

6

Finance and investment

This chapter covers the basic financial concepts that every non-financial manager should understand. Most of the calculations to do with investment and finance involve two important ideas: *interest* and *inflation*. In this chapter we will look at both in some detail, and at indexing, which is a powerful way to summarise financial data:

- Points to watch out for in financial data.
- Interest.
- Inflation.
- Payback.
- Discounted cashflow.
- Finding the future value of a stream of payments.
- Indexing.
- More on interest rates.

Points to watch out for in financial data

We don't always have enough time to check all the financial information that we are faced with, but when making a decision that involves a large sum of money, it's worth taking the trouble to consider whether you can rely on the figures you have been given. Ask yourself:

- *Is there any sign of conscious bias?* Are any of the statements ambiguous or clearly untrue? For instance, do the results talk about averages in some cases and then switch to a specific kind of average (mean, median or mode) in other cases? Check the other averages to see if they produce different results.

■ *Has unfavourable information been ignored?* Who has produced the information and what motive might they have for interpreting it in a certain way?

■ *Is there any sign of unconscious bias?* In the UK, estate agents generally want to show that the market in private homes is improving. They may honestly be trying to be objective with their figures, but, nevertheless, they may be overlooking certain factors. The same goes for politicians, special interest groups, economists and many others. Watch out for the use of highly respected institutions such as medical organisations and universities being associated with results. Has the institution interpreted the results, or has someone else made the interpretation using the institution's data?

■ *How representative is the sample?* Is it large enough? Is the sample assumed to represent more than one population?

■ *In a reported correlation, how big was the sample?* If it is stated that A caused B, could B have conceivably caused A? Is the standard error given? In many cases, the answers to these questions are enough to reject inferences regarding cause and effect as unproven.

Reported figures may not be the same as actual figures. Economic data from many developing countries, for instance, are often highly unreliable. Another example is crime statistics. For example, if a rape is not reported, as is often the case, then it won't appear in the statistics. The same effect occurs when people are asked questions that they do not wish to answer truthfully. What they say they do is not the same as what they actually do. Can we believe people's statements regarding tax evasion, for instance?

All forecasts and extrapolations should be regarded with caution. In the early seventies we were told that oil would have run out by now; it hasn't. Predictions about the future are guesses, not facts. Try to find out as much as possible about how the prediction was arrived at.

A note on percentages and percentiles

If you have made a 2% profit on an investment in one year and a 4% profit in the next, you can describe it in different ways depending on the impression you want to give. If you want to make it sound small, you can say the second year profit rose by 2 percentage points. If you want to make it sound bigger, you can say profits in the second year rose by 100%.

If there are 100 employees earning salaries all of which are different amounts, the highest earner is in the ninety-ninth percentile, the next highest earner is in the ninety-eighth percentile, and so on. Suppose 90 employees earn less than £20,000 a year; if you make comparisons by looking at which percentile a person is in, suggesting that the difference between the salary of the person in the ninety-fourth percentile and the one in the eighty-ninth is similar to the difference between those in the fifty-fourth and forty-ninth percentiles would be quite wrong. Percentiles just tell you about the order of things, not about the amount of difference between them.

Real-life stories   **You just can't reason with some people**

As anyone who deals with customers knows, there are some people who just won't listen to reason. This often occurs in the investment world. We should have a little sympathy for the stockbrokers and financial advisers who sometimes have to deal with loopy investors who have mad theories about how investment works and won't be persuaded otherwise.

There have always been people who ignore mathematical proofs, and there always will be. Take the problem of squaring a circle. It can be proved that it is impossible geometrically to construct a square that has exactly the same area as a given circle. This proof has not deterred circle-squarers, however, who continue to try to show that it can be done.

In 1849 a man wrote to the Lord Chancellor demanding a £100,000 reward for his proof that a circle could be squared (no such reward had been offered). August De Morgan, a mathematician, was instructed to write to the man explaining that he was wrong. The man wrote back recommending that De Morgan 'change his business and appropriate his time and attention to a Sunday School to learn what he could and keep the little children from durting their close' [sic], and signed his letter, 'With sincere feelings of gratitude for your weakness and inability, I am, Sir, your superior in mathematics.'

These days, irrational customers don't seem to write such stylish letters!

Interest

Interest is a price paid for having the use of someone else's money. The price is mainly based on the time you keep the money. If you borrow money from, say, a bank, you will usually pay interest at a rate expressed as x% per year. Likewise, if you deposit a sum of money with a bank or building society, you are in effect lending them the money, and you want to receive some interest as payment. In theory, if you deposit £100 in a savings account for a year and the interest rate is 10% per annum, after 12 months you can withdraw all the money and the interest, and you will have a total of £110.

There are a number of complications to this simple picture. The first is taxation. In many countries, including the UK, interest is taxed at source by the government, so the bank has to deduct the tax and send it directly to the government. In the UK, currently the rule is that 20% of interest is deducted at source, so at a 10% interest rate, you would only receive £8 on your £100 deposit. If you are not due to pay tax, you must claim the other 20% of the interest back from the government.

A second complication is the effect of changes to the buying power of money (inflation and deflation). This is examined in more detail later in this chapter, but for now you should note that usually your £100 will buy fewer goods and services in a year's time than it can today. So part of the interest you receive should compensate you for the drop in the buying power of your £100.

Banks and building societies are powerful commercial organizations, so they are in a position to charge consumers quite high interest rates when a consumer borrows money, and to pay much lower interest rates to consumers who deposit money with them. Quite often, after you take into account the tax deductions and the drop in the buying power of money, you will find that you are only getting a 'real' interest rate of a fraction of 1%, or, worse still, that the real interest rate is negative, as occurred in early 2011. For this reason, many people prefer to keep their money in other investments that can be easily sold for cash, but offer, over a longer period, a better real rate of return than bank deposits.

Simple interest

Simple interest is when you leave your deposit for a period of time, say five years, but withdraw the interest each year. If you deposit £100 in a bank for five years at 10% simple interest a year, you would earn £10 interest per year (let's ignore tax and inflation for now):

Year 1	10
Year 2	10
Year 3	10
Year 4	10
Year 5	10
Total	£50

At the end of the fifth year you could get your original £100 back. You will also have received £50 interest during the period, totalling £150. The value of the £100 when you first make the deposit can be called the 'present value', and the value of what you will have in five years' time (£150) can be called the 'future value'.

Simple interest in real life: hire purchase agreements

Simple interest is much rarer than compound interest (see below), to the extent that many people think that it is just a textbook concept. However, it does occasionally occur in financing deals, such as hire purchase agreements. Hire purchase agreements are schemes where you purchase an item from a shop, financed by a hire purchase loan, and repay the loan plus interest over time. The catch is that in some agreements the lender charges simple interest on the original price of the item over the entire period of the loan, instead of reducing the amount of interest gradually as you pay down the loan; this has the effect of increasing the total amount of interest you pay. These types of schemes are on the way out.

Compound interest

If you lend a bank £100 for five years by making a deposit, and the bank promises to pay interest at 10% a year, you can leave the interest in the account so that you can earn interest on the interest. This is called 'compound interest'.

Deposit	£100
First year's interest	£10
Total at end of year 1	£110
Second year's interest on £110	£11
Total at end of year 2	£121

Compound interest doesn't look like much of an improvement in the early years, but over time it makes a big difference. Look what happens after 10, 15 and 20 years:

Deposit	Total after 10 yrs	Total after 15 yrs	Total after 20 yrs
100	259.37	417.72	672.75

There are a number of issues that complicate this, which will be examined later, but you can see the principle here: over time, the amount you accumulate through the compounding effect becomes the major part of the asset.

Investments such as shares don't pay interest (although they may sometimes pay dividends, but these tend to be a small proportion of the investment gains), but when you compare different kinds of investments, you consider their returns; in the case of an investment that accumulates interest, the interest is called the 'return', and in the case of other investments, the total overall gain that you make, which may include dividend payments and an increase in the market value of the asset, is called the return.

Inflation

Inflation is usually defined as a general increase in prices over time. Its opposite is deflation, defined as a general decrease in prices over time. While the causes of inflation are complex and not fully understood by economists, the general consensus is that a low, steady rate of inflation is the most preferable state, because it is easier to keep the economy stable under these conditions. It's worth noting that inflation isn't a new phenomenon. For example, throughout history, kings have occasionally resorted to minting coins with less gold in them than before and passing them off as the same value; this gave them a gain in the short term, because they could use the debased coins to pay their bills and thus make their gold go further. However, people tend to discover quite quickly that a coin has been debased, and will tend to raise their prices to compensate for this, which has an inflationary effect. Debasing the coinage affected the supply of money in circulation. Today, controlling the money supply is one of the main ways that central banks try to influence the inflation.

As we saw earlier, if you have £100 today, and the inflation rate is 10% this year, in a year's time your £100 will only buy what £90 could buy today. Thus, you can treat inflation in the same way as compound interest when you are accounting for it. The future inflation rate is never known precisely, so your calculations will never be exactly right. The inflation rates published by governments are based on samples; so not only is it impossible to know future inflation rates precisely, but also it is usually impossible to know if the published current inflation rate actually applies accurately to what you want to spend your money on.

The real rate of return

The 'real' rate of return refers to the rate you obtain after accounting for inflation and, in some cases, taxation and other charges. Because in most cases nobody knows exactly what the future inflation rate will be, measuring what the real rate of return on an investment at some point in the future will be only produces an estimate. You can only work out real rate precisely for periods that have already occurred. Nevertheless, investment professionals like to adjust returns for inflation to make them comparable, so in general it is the 'real rate' that they are talking about.

So what kind of 'real return' is a good rate of return? Although a lot of companies talk big about permanently high rates of return (say 20% or more), the reality is that over the long term, on average, public companies listed on the stock market do not reach anything like this figure; depending on the country, the average return over the long term is more like 5–7% a year. Private companies tend to do worse, especially if you include the countless small businesses that fail to make adequate profits. A 'real' rate of return of 5–7% may not look like much, but it is more than you can obtain on average in the long term from other types of investment, such as cash deposits and government bonds. There are, of course, exceptional companies that do much better than this for a long time, but they are the exceptions, not the general rule.

Fixed-term investments

It is also important to compare the other terms of different investments, because you can make more or less money depending on the terms, even if the annual interest rates are the same.

Example

Suppose you can lend £1,000 to a bank for a year for 8% interest, or to another bank for six months at the same rate. Which is better? If you had no other way of lending the money, you would have to consider the following:

■ Can you withdraw the money before the period is up? Are there 'penalties' (e.g. loss of interest) for doing so?

■ Do you think that interest rates are likely to change during the period in which you invest the money? You probably won't know for certain, but you might be able to make a guess if you read the financial pages regularly.

If both the investments are for fixed terms, and you can't take the money out again before the end of the period, it might be better to lend for six months than for a year, so you could do something else with the money for the second six months. If, however, you thought that by the end of the six months banks would only be paying 6% interest on new deposits, you would be better off lending for a whole year, since for the second half of the year you would be getting 2% more interest than the going rate. Many cash and near-cash investments let you take out money whenever you want, which is a benefit for which you often pay a price, in the form of a lower interest rate than if you tied the money up for a fixed term.

Comparing investments part 1: payback

There are many ways to compare investments, as we will see later, but one simple rule-of-thumb measure is used surprisingly often: 'payback'.

Suppose you have invested £100,000 in a business venture for five years. You have been paid back out of profits annually, and by the end of the five years you have got your capital back and some profit. The annual returns were:

	Paid back
Year 1	£1,000
Year 2	£5,000
Year 3	£10,000
Year 4	£80,000
Year 5	£150,000
Total	£246,000

Subtracting your initial £100,000 from the total of £246,000 leaves you with £146,000. Assuming inflation rates have been low, you don't need to do a lot of complicated analysis to see quickly that: (1) the returns have been pretty good, and (2) you didn't claw back all the money you originally invested until year 5, although you got most of it back by the end of year 4.

Suppose you had invested another £100,000 at the same time into a different venture, and the returns were:

	Paid back
Year 1	£10,000
Year 2	£150,000
Year 3	£1,000
Year 4	£80,000
Year 5	£5,000
Total	£246,000

You would have got exactly the same amount, £2,460,000, at the end, but in the second business you would have got £150,000 back in the second year, so you would already have made a handsome profit. As we have already seen, in the first venture you would not have got all your capital back until the final year. Which business has proved to be the better investment?

To answer that sensibly, we would need to have realistic estimates of how the two businesses were likely to perform in future years, and how much further investment they might need to keep them going. Let's suppose, that the first business involved marketing a new specialist product that had reached all the potential buyers by year 5 and that orders are likely to plummet in year 6, and that the second business was a yacht builder who built two luxury yachts for two millionaire friends during the five years and is now unable to find any more customers. Since neither of the businesses has a good future, which investment has been better? Many people would say that the second investment has been better, because the investors got their money back in year 2, three years before the first investment did the same; in other words, the second business had a quicker payback.

Payback is a primitive way to assess investments, but it often produces results that are a good approximation of much more sophisticated methods. It is appropriate for relatively risky ventures where the long-term outlook is going to be difficult to control, and where the investors do not want to go on pouring money into a business to keep it going. The prospect of getting your money back quite quickly is extremely attractive to investors, and it is easy for them to say 'yes' to such projects, assuming that they judge the income projections to be realistic. It is not the only way, or even the best way, to assess investment potential, but it has its place, especially in circumstances that require quick decisions.

Test yourself: Part 8

1 During the 1980s and 1990s, Brazil suffered from very high levels of inflation, called 'hyperinflation'. In 1994, for example, the inflation rate was 2,075.8%. Many people were simply too poor to be part of the consumer society, and survived by subsistence farming. Others who received an income struggled to save money. What methods do you think people with a small income, but who had no access to international financial markets, adopted to try to prevent their savings from becoming worthless?

2 Some companies listed on the world's stock markets have a policy of paying regular dividends to their investors. Why do you think this might be, and why might some investors not like this policy?

3 Can you think of any reasons why payback might not be an adequate method of comparing the performance of two investments?

See page 203 for the answers.

Comparing investments part 2: discounted cash flow

Discounted cash flow (DCF) is a method of estimating the value of any investment by expressing all the sums of money it is expected to generate in the future in today's money and adding them together. Usually, the sums of money used to calculate DCF are those that the investment generates after paying for all expenses and the cost of replacing essential equipment.

To understand why we need to convert the future income into today's money, i.e. its 'present value', consider the following:

Fred asks you to lend him £10,000 interest-free. When you ask Fred when he will pay you back, he offers you two choices: either he will pay you back next week, or he will pay you back in three years' time. Which option do you prefer?

The sensible choice, from your point of view, is to choose to be repaid next week, because then you will get the money back soon and be able to do something useful with it, such as investing it at a good rate of interest. If you lend Fred the money for three years interest free, you will lose the interest you could have earned, and you will also have incurred the risk that for whatever reason Fred does not pay you back when the money becomes due. In other words, the length of time for which you commit a sum of money has a value – and in investment parlance, this is known as the 'time value' of money. We can quantify and compare different investments by estimating their present value using various formulae, such as:

$$\text{Present value} = \text{The future value of a sum of money} \div (1 + \text{Interest rate})^{n \,=\, \text{number of years}}$$

which can be applied when there is a single repayment in the future.

To calculate the present value of the loan repayment in three years' time, you need to 'discount' the future value, which in this case is £10,000, by an appropriate rate of interest. Suppose interest rates for three year deposits are currently around 5%. You can decide to use a rate of 5% in your formula. Alternatively, you could decide to choose a higher rate that you think compensates you for the risk that Fred doesn't pay you back, or doesn't pay you back on time, but since Fred doesn't want to pay interest, that would be merely theoretical.

At a 5% discount rate,

$$\text{Present value} = 10{,}000 \div (1 + 0.05)^3$$
$$= 10{,}000 \div [(1.05) \times (1.05) \times (1.05)]$$
$$= 10{,}000 \div 1.158$$
$$= 8{,}635.58$$

The present value, or PV, gives you a measurement of how much money you will lose by making this interest-free loan, compared with putting it in an interest-bearing deposit for three years.

The risk-free rate

Even if you deposit money in a savings account it may not be completely safe, as savers in Icesave, a brand of the Icelandic bank Landsbanki, discovered in 2008 when the bank collapsed (UK savers did receive compensation, but from the UK government, not Iceland). The same is true of government bonds: you cannot be 100% certain that even the British government, which has never defaulted on its bonds since they were introduced in the 1700s, may not default on its debt obligations (such as bonds) at some point in the future.

Nevertheless, if we want to assess the merits of an investment that we know carries some risk, it is useful to have a 'risk-free' rate of interest to compare it with. Professional investors often use the rate available on short-dated government bonds as a proxy for the risk-free rate. Knowing that you can obtain, say, a 2% real return risk-free helps you to decide whether a more risky investment is going to yield a return that is worth the risk. At the very least, it tells you that the return should be higher than 2%.

Assessing companies using DCF

As we saw in Chapter 4, it becomes more and more difficult to make accurate forecasts the further you go into the future. This means that if you attempt to use DCF to estimate the value of cash flows to a company more than two or three years into the future, you are likely to be way off the mark, especially in the later years. The range of DCF calculations you can make is very wide, and many of them are extremely elaborate, but ultimately they all depend on the assumptions and judgements made by the person doing the analysis.

In spite of this, many investment professionals regard the DCF method as the best way to estimate the value of a company. It tends to produce more conservative valuations than other methods, which is prudent, and it forces analysts to focus on each item of future cash flow and ask themselves, 'Do I really believe that this is likely to happen?', which other methods tend not to do. Another advantage is that DCF allows you to disregard any consideration of what the market for selling your investment might be in the future: DCF requires you to look at a business solely in terms of the cash you estimate that it will generate over a period of years, and value it on that basis. This helps to protect you from absurdities like the ones that occurred during the dotcom boom of the 1990s and early 2000s, when many internet-based companies were trading on the stock market at colossal valuations despite making no profits at all. The biggest dotcom failure, Webvan, was an online grocery service in the US, which was launched on the stockmarket in 2000 and went bust owing $800 million in 2001, having spectacularly failed to meet its sales targets or to make a profit. Like many other dotcom failures, Webvan had made unrealistic assumptions about how much of the market for its products it could capture, and how quickly it could do it. A steely-eyed analyst who used DCF to examine these assumptions, and knew something about the grocery business, would not have been carried away by the claims that the firm could attract vast numbers of customers very quickly.

Example

Calculate the cumulative 'net present value' (NPV), which is the sum of all the present values in the forecast, for Steadyco PLC from the forecasts below, using a discount rate of 10%.

$$\text{Cumulative NPV} = \text{the sum of all terms } R_t \div (1 + i)^t$$

where R = the amount of cash received in time period t
t = the time period
i = the discount rate

We can make this calculation a bit easier by working out the factor for each time period first, by substituting 1 for R in the formula. So, for example, the factor for year 1 will be:

$$R_1 \div (1 + 0.1)^1 = 1 \div 1.1 = 0.9091$$

The factors for years 2 to 5 will be:

Year 2 factor = $1 \div (1 + 0.1)^2 = 1 \div 1.21$ = 0.8264
Year 3 factor = $1 \div (1 + 0.1)^3 = 1 \div 1.331$ = 0.7513
Year 4 factor = $1 \div (1 + 0.1)^4 = 1 \div 1.4641$ = 0.6830
Year 5 factor = $1 \div (1 + 0.1)^5 = 1 \div 1.61051$ = 0.6209

Now all we have to do is multiply the cash flow for each period by the factor for that period:

	Cash flow	Factor	NPV
	Steadyco profit forecast		
Year 1	200,000	0.9091	181,820
Year 2	200,000	0.8264	165,280
Year 3	200,000	0.7513	150,260
Year 4	200,000	0.6830	136,600
Year 5	200,000	0.6209	124,180
Total NPV			758,140

Other uses of present value

Once you begin to get the hang of this method, you can rearrange it to perform other types of calculations that are variations on the theme. For example, suppose you are a high-earner and you want to send your child to a fee-paying school in eight years' time. The school has guaranteed you that the fees will be fixed at £15,000 a year for the five years that the child will be there; how much should you save every month at 10% a year compounded monthly to generate £15,000 for each of the five years of schooling?

First, we have to work out the total amount of money you have to save by the time the child goes to school. This is done by working out the PV (present value) of the school fees at that point, in 8 years' time, this time using the formula in the form:

$$PV = p \times [\{1 - (I + i)^{-n}\} \div i]$$

where p is the monthly amount of annual school fee, n is the number of monthly periods during the five years of school and i is the interest rate per monthly period, assuming that the same interest rate of 10% a year is sustained.

$$p = 15,000 \div 12 = 1,250$$
$$n = 60$$
$$i = 0.1 \div 12 = 0.00833$$

$$PV = 1{,}250 \times [\{1 - (1 + 0.00833)^{-60}\} \div 0.00833]$$
$$= 1{,}250 \times [\{1 - 1.00833^{-60}\} \div 0.00833]$$
$$= 1{,}250 \times [(1 - 0.6079) \div 0.00833]$$
$$= 1{,}250 \times (0.3921 \div 0.00833)$$
$$= 1{,}250 \times 47.0708$$
$$= 58{,}838.50$$

Now we work out how much you have to save a month for the next eight years to have £58,838.50 at the time when your child starts school. To do this we use the formula:

$$p = (A \times i) \div [(1 + i)^n - 1]$$

where p is the amount you have to save every month, A is the 'annuity', or the amount of money you must have at the time when your child starts school, i is the interest rate per period and n is the number of periods.

$$A = 58{,}838.50$$
$$i = 0.1 \div 12 = 0.00833$$
$$n = 96$$

$$p = (58{,}838.50 \times 0.00833) \div [(1 + 0.00833)^{96} - 1]$$
$$= 490.1247 \div (2.2175 - 1)$$
$$= 402.5665$$

You will have to save £402.57 a month until the child goes to school.

Finding the future value of a stream of payments

Any financial arrangement where a fixed investment of money is paid at regular intervals is an 'annuity'. You may have heard of annuities in connection with pensions, where a pensioner pays over a large cash sum to an insurance company in return for a guarantee of being paid a fixed smaller sum each year for the rest of their lives. The payments to the pensioner consist of repayments of portions of the principal plus interest. It is a type of gamble, since if you live until you are, say, 120 years old, you will get much more back than if you live until you are, say, 66. The insurance companies calculate the repayment sums based on what they know about the average life spans of the general population.

The regular payments from an annuity are called a stream of payments. Sinking funds and mortgage repayments work on a similar principle. In all these cases, the payments will eventually stop.

Sometimes wealthy individuals leave a large sum to a charity. For instance, someone may leave money to a university to help impecunious students work on a particular subject. The money is often invested to provide regular sums out of the interest alone, which is an example of a 'perpetual annuity', where the payments never cease.

To work out the future value of a stream of payments, imagine that you are saving £1,000 a year for four years, at which point you will buy a car. Suppose that the effective rate (see page 145) is 4% p.a., and that you pay in the £1,000 at the end of each year.

The first thing to notice is that the £1,000 you pay in year 4 won't earn any interest because you are taking it straight out again. The year 1 payment will earn interest for years 2, 3 and 4, which is:

$$FV = 1,000 \times 1.04^3 = 1,124.86$$

The year 2 payment will earn interest for years 3 and 4:

$$FV = 1,000 \times 1.04^2 = 1,081.60$$

The year 3 payment will earn interest for year 4 only:

$$FV = 1,000 \times 1.04 = 1,040$$

Adding the FVs for all four payments together, we get:

$$FV = 1,124.86 + 1,081.60 + 1,081.60 + 1,040 = 4,246.46$$

Suppose you decide to make the payments at the beginning of the year instead of at the end:

Start of year 1   1,000
Start of year 2   1,000
Start of year 3   1,000
Start of year 4   1,000

Work out the FVs for each year in the same way as before:

$$FV1 = 1,000 \times 1.04^4 = 1,169.86$$
$$FV2 = 1,000 \times 1.04^3 = 1,124.86$$
$$FV3 = 1,000 \times 1.04^2 = 1,081.60$$
$$FV4 = 1,000 \times 1.04 = 1,040.00$$

$$\text{Total FV} = 1,169.86 + 1,124.86 + 1,081.60 + 1,040 = 4,416.32$$

The general formula for calculating the future value of a stream of payments (where payment is at the end of the period) is:

$$FV = p \times [(l + i)^n \div i]$$

where p is the amount of the regular payment per period, n is the number of periods and i is the interest rate per period.

Indexing

Now that we have delved into the fundamental method for working out streams of payments in various forms we should turn to indexing, which is very widely used in economics, finance and investment. These days almost everyone encounters reports that use indices, but many people remain hazy about what they really mean. This section shows how this simple but powerful tool is calculated.

An index number is a summary of a quantity of data, often obtained by sampling. We will need to remember the statistical ideas we looked at in Chapters 1 and 2 in order to understand indexing properly. In the UK, the Office for National Statistics (ONS) publishes a monthly Consumer Price Index (CPI) as a guide to the changes in the cost of living. It also publishes a host of other publications, such as the *Monthly Digest of Statistics* which contains indices of many facets of the economy.

Probably the best known index in the UK is the one mentioned above, the Consumer Price Index, which attempts to show changes in the cost of living for the average person. It is based on the prices of a large number of goods and services, compared with the prices for the same things at a previous period. To produce the index, the Office for National Statistics does not record the price of every single product and service that is sold at every possible outlet in the UK – it takes samples of a range of products and services. There is some controversy over whether the CPI is sufficiently representative, and there have been accusations that it can be manipulated for political purposes, but it is generally accepted as a useful measure of inflation. Like other indices, such as the Producer Price Index, which measures the relative prosperity of businesses between two periods, not all the experts agree on the actual prices and quantities that should be used. This is largely because they are very hard to measure. According to the ONS, researchers visit about 150 outlets around the UK every month to collect about 110,000 prices for 560 different goods and services. They visit the same places each month so that they are comparing like for like when registering price changes.

Calculating the change

So, how does this information translate into an index? When comparing, say, annual price levels, one particular year is taken as the 'base' year, and other years are compared with it. The convention is to write the base year as P0 and the year you are comparing it with as P1. If just one item is in the index, such as orange juice, the difference, or 'price relative', is calculated as:

$$\text{Price relative} = (P1 \div P0) \times 100$$

Example

If your base year is 2000, and the price of orange juice then was 0.75 a litre, and in 2015 it is 1.85 a litre, the price relative is $(1.85 \div 0.75)) \times 100 = 246.66$.

Subtracting 100 from the price relative gives you the percentage increase over the period. The percentage increase in the price of orange juice in our example of the 15-year period between 2000 and 2015 (not real data) is $246.66 - 100 = 146.66\%$.

In some widely published indices, the average of several consecutive years is used as the base year, so it would be more correct to describe it as a 'base period' than a 'base year'. Sometimes it is better to include the quantity of an item sold in the index, since it tells you how much is being sold, and also, if you have several items in the index, it gives you an idea of which ones are the most important.

Multiplying the quantity of an item sold by its unit price gives you the value of the total quantity sold. This measurement is called the 'value relative', and the formula for it is:

$$\text{Value relative at Time 1} = [(Q1 \times P1) \div (Q0 \times P0)] \times 100$$

where Time 1 is the year you are comparing with the base year, Q1 is the quantity sold at Time 1, P1 is the price at Time 1, Q0 is the quantity sold in the base year and P0 is the price at the base year.

Example

You want to know how the price of petrol and the average quantity of orange juice used per head (per capita) has changed in 2015 compared with your base year of 2000. In other words, you want to know the value relative. The prices are the same as in the previous example, and the quantity sold per capita in 2015 is 270 litres, and in 2000 is 204 litres. Using the value relative formula,

$$\begin{aligned}\text{Value relative at 2015} &= [(270 \times 1.85) \div (204 \times 0.75)] \times 100 \\ &= (499.50 \div 253) \times 100 \\ &= 197.43\end{aligned}$$

the percentage increase for the period is $197.43 - 100 = 97.43\%$.

Weighted aggregate index

Suppose you want to compare the value relative of four basic food items, milk, bread, mince and potatoes, in 2015 and 2000. Table 6.1 shows the notional prices and quantities. To get the total value of the 'basket' of four foods in each year, you add the value of each food together, as has been done in the table.

Table 6.1 Imaginary prices and quantities for four foods consumed per capita (2000, 2015)

	2000			2015		
Food	Quantity	Price		Quantity	Price	
	Q0	P0	Value	Q1	P1	Value
Bread	60 lb	0.67	40.20	53 lb	1.95	103.35
Mince	31 lb	0.99	30.69	70 lb	2.20	154.00
Potato	70 lb	0.51	35.70	61 lb	1.20	73.20
Milk	100 ltr	0.15	15.00	79 ltr	0.89	70.31
			121.59			400.86

The total value in 2000 is 121.59, and the total value in 2015 is 400.86, so the percentage change in 2015 from 2000 is:

$$[(400.86 \div 121.59) \times 100] - 100 = 229.68\%.$$

This kind of index is called a 'weighted index' because each price has been multiplied by a 'weight', in this case, quantity consumed per capita. Its full name is a 'weighted aggregate index' because it considers the 'aggregate', or total, of several items.

Calculating the Consumer Price Index and the Retail Price Index in the UK

The two principal indices used to measure inflation in the UK are the Consumer Price Index (CPI) and the Retail Price Index (RPI). The Bank of England uses the CPI to measure if the economy is keeping to inflation targets set by the government, and it is used for comparisons with price indices of other countries. The RPI has a longer history than the CPI, and until 2011 was used to set the rates of index-linked state benefits, pensions, government bonds and customs duties. Since April 2011, the CPI is being been used for this purpose, with some exceptions, such as government bonds, which are still linked to the RPI.

These indices provide a measure of the average change across a range of consumer purchases. They are weighted to reflect the greater importance of some items than others. For example, petrol is a major item of expense for most people, so it is given greater weight than, say, salt. The CPI's weights are calculated differently from the RPI's weights; the CPI aims to represent the spending of all consumers in the UK, including foreign visitors, while the RPI aims to represent the typical household. Every year, the components of the indices are reviewed and adjusted in an effort to keep them representative, and are then fixed until the following year. The same is done with the weighting. This is important, because consumers do change what they spend their money on over time. For example, in recent years people have spent a much large proportion of their income on travel and electronics than they did in the past.

We have already seen that the CPI and RPI aim to represent slightly different things (all consumer spending versus the typical household). Some other important differences are that the CPI does not include expenditure related to accommodation, such as mortgage payments and council tax (this has been criticised), and the CPI uses the geometric mean while the RPI uses the arithmetic mean in the early stages of calculation.

The CPI and RPI are often called the 'headline' indices, perhaps because they are the ones usually used in newspaper headlines about inflation. They are useful as generalised measures, but if you want to examine inflation in, say, a particular market, you will need to use a more specialised index. As well as the CPI and RPI, the Office for National Statistics publishes a large number of more specialised indices for this purpose.

The base year for the CPI is 2005, which is given the value of 100. If the CPI in February 2014 is 123, it would mean that you would have to spend £123 then to purchase the same amount of goods and services that you could have bought for £100 in 2005. The base year for the RPI is 1987. From time to time the base years may change (for example, the RPI started in 1947).

Why is the base year changed sometimes?

As time passes, CPIs have to change the base year that they use, because prices increase so much. For example, the CPI in the US was 217.4 in 1979, and 195.4 in 1978, using 1967 as the base year. 217.4 − 195.4 = 22, so you would be technically correct to say that the index went up by 22 points between 1978 and 1979, but your listeners might think you meant that the index went up by 22%. This is an example of the 'percentage of what?' problem discussed on page 195. It went up by 22% of the *base year* prices, not last year's prices. We are more interested in how much it went up as a percentage of the 1978 prices. To do this, we subtract 100 from the value relative in 1978:

$$\text{Value relative at 1979} = [(217.4 \div 195.4) \times 100 = 112.5$$
$$112.5 - 100 = 12.5$$

The percentage increase in prices from 1978 to 1979 was 12.5%, not 22%. To lessen the chances of making this mistake, the base years of CPIs are often changed to keep the index under 200. If the index is 110, you can see the percentage increase from the base year at a glance. Choosing a base year is difficult because it must be an 'ordinary' sort of year when nothing unusual happened, otherwise it would not be representative.

Purchasing power

We often hear people talking about their currency being worth a fraction of what it was worth at an earlier date. It is easy to work this out for yourself. The formula is:

$$\text{Purchasing power} = (1 \div \text{CPI}) \times 100.$$

If the base year of the CPI for, say, Japan, is 2000, and the index in 2005 is, say, 117, the yen in 2005 is worth $(1 \div 117) \times 100 - 85\%$ of what it was worth in 2000.

Splicing the indices

As we have seen, as well as changing the base year, the weighting of a price index must also often be changed, with new items added to the list of goods and services to reflect changes in a society's buying patterns. When this is done, the index may change to a number which doesn't look like the old numbers at all, so it must be adjusted to blend with the old index numbers. This is done by multiplying the new numbers by a number which makes the new index equal the old index in the year that the change is made, and is called 'splicing' the index numbers.

Example

Suppose there is an index with a base year of 2000, and the weights are changed in 2005. The old index looks like this:

2000	100
2001	109
2002	112
2003	116
2004	118
2005	122

After the weights are changed in 2005, the 2005 index is 96.8. To get the ratio of this number to the old index number, divide the old number by the new one:

$$122 \div 96.8 = 1.26$$

$1.26 \times 96.8 = 122$, so if you multiply the new index by 1.26 for 2005 and every subsequent year, you have given continuity to the index series, or 'spliced' the numbers.

Shifting bases and indices

Consider the following statement: 'Our market share dropped last year by 33% from the year before. This year our market share has increased by 11%, clawing back a third of last year's loss.'

This may appear to be true, but it isn't. If the market share in 2013 is 60%, and in 2014 it drops to 40% (a loss of 33%), the 11% increase in 2015 is 11% of 40%, which is 4.4%, bringing the market share back to 44.4%; this is not the same as 'clawing back' a third of the loss of 2014, which is a third of 20% = 6.67%, and would make the 2015 share 46.67%, not the real figure of 44.4%.

What has happened is that the statement has confused two different bases, which is a common error. The 2014 decrease uses the 2013 market share as the base. The 2015 increase uses the 2014 market share as a base, which is a smaller figure.

Indices are also a fertile ground for the deliberate twister of facts. Let's take a very simplified price index to show how this is done. Suppose the figures are as shown in Table 6.2.

Table 6.2 Price per unit for two items (2014, 2015)

Item	2014 price per unit	2015 price per unit
Bread	0.50	1.00
Cheese	1.00	0.50

If you take 2014 as the base period, setting it at 100, you could say that in 2015 bread went up to 200, and cheese went down to 50 as in Table 6.3.

Table 6.3 Price index: 2014 base period

Item	2014	2015
Bread	100	200
Cheese	100	50
Average	100	125

You can also say that prices (meaning average prices) have gone up by 25%. Now let's try it with 2015 as the base period (see Table 6.4).

Table 6.4 Price index: 2015 base period

Item	2014	2015
Bread	50	100
Cheese	200	100
Average	125	100

Now you can say that prices have gone down by 25%. You have been telling the truth both times, but the naive reader is liable to believe the statement of increase or decrease without looking more closely at what it really means.

More on interest rates

Tho convei siun periòd

How much compound interest you receive depends on how often the bank gives you the interest. If you deposit £2 million in a bank at 10% p.a. and it only gives you the interest at the end of the year, you would have £200,000 in interest at the end of the year, but what if it calculated the interest every six months? The annual interest rate would be the same, but the interest you earned in the first six months, half of £200,000 = £100,000, would earn interest during the second half of the year. You would earn an extra £5,000, which is half of 10% of £100,000. The interval between the times when the bank calculates the interest is called the 'conversion period'. The shorter the conversion period, the more the interest will be compounded, and the more money you will make at a given annual rate.

The accumulation factor

When you look at interest rates offered for deposits, you need to know the conversion period as well as the rate. If the interest rate is 10% p.a. with two conversion periods it means that the interest is calculated every six months. For each of those six months, the total of capital and interest on £1 invested is 1 ÷ (0.1 ÷ 2) = 1.05. This is called the 'accumulation factor'. If you invest £1,000, you multiply it by the accumulation factor to get the total you will have at the end of one conversion period:

$$1,000 \times 1.05 = 1,050.$$

To work out the total at the end of two conversion periods (in this case, two six-month periods), you multiply the sum invested by the accumulation factor twice:

$$1,000 \times 1.05 \times 1.05 = 1,102.50.$$

Suppose there are 12 conversion periods; the accumulation factor is 1 ÷ (0.1 ÷ 12)= 1.00833 per month. At the end of six months, the £1,000 will be worth:

$$1,000 \times 1.00833 \times 1.00833 \times 1.00833 \times 1.00833 \times 1.00833 \times 1.00833.$$

This is a bit long-winded, but the sum is easier if we write it in the form $1,000 \times 1.00833^6$. We write the accumulation factor to the power of six because we are multiplying it by itself six times. Remember that you can use a calculator to get powers:

$$1,000 \times 1.00833^6 = 1,051.03.$$

£1,051.03 may not seem much more than the £1,050 we got when we worked out the total for a six-month conversion period, but if you were investing millions, it would be a significant amount. For this reason it's important to examine closely how interest is calculated when dealing with large sums.

Suppose inflation is 5% a year; how much money would you have to keep under the bed (without earning any interest on it) in order to have £100,000 worth of spending power in today's money in five years' time? The accumulation factor is 1 + (0.05 ÷ 1) = 1.05. Raising the accumulation factor to the power of 5, for the five years, we get:

$$1.05^1 = 1.2763, \text{ or } 27.63\%.$$

You would have to put £127,630 under the bed to have £100,000 worth of spending power in five years' time.

Suppose you don't like the idea of inflation eating into your money, so you decide to put the £100,000 into a bank. You might find that you could only get 4% interest a year (adjusted to one conversion period), so inflation would still be eating into your money. You could calculate the annual rate of change in the value of your money in the bank as:

$$1 - (1.04 \div 1.05) = 1 - 0.9904 = 0.0096$$

Your spending power is shrinking by 0.96% (less than 1%) a year. Don't subtract the inflation rate from the interest rate, or vice versa, because it will give you a wrong answer, which in this case is 1% exactly. This is due to the fact that this method doesn't take compounding into account.

Inflation rates are never certain, so if you know an FV and you want to work out the PV, taking inflation into account, you have to guess the inflation rate. Suppose you will be paid £50,000 in three years' time and you estimate that the inflation rate will be 2% in the first year, 4% in the second year and 5% in the third year.

The accumulation factor for three years is $1.02 \times 1.04 \times 1.05 = 1.1138$, so the present value of £50,000 received in three years' time is:

$$PV = 50,000 \div 1.1138 = 44,891.36$$

Remember that this is only an estimate, so if you make a calculation like this in a report, always state your assumptions about inflation rates clearly.

Are there 365 days in year?

Not if you can get away with having a different number! Interest on bonds, for example, which is usually compounded daily, is based on some peculiar views of the calendar:

- In many countries, the interest on bonds is calculated on the basis that there are 30 days in every month, giving 360 days to a year.
- Many bonds in the US also give interest on a 360-day year basis, but give you an extra day's interest if you invest on the 30th of a month and take the money back on the thirty-first of another month.

What about leap years? Every fourth year, there is an extra day, 29 February.

- In Japan and the UK, most bonds issuers accept that there are 365 days in a year, but they still calculate 365 days' interest in a leap year.
- There are some bonds that do agree that there are 366 days in a leap year.

The amount that you lose by having, say, 360 days in a year instead of 365 is tiny, so long as the daily rate is calculated as rate ÷ 360. Something to watch for, though, is whether the conversion periods turn out to be of different lengths, which would result in the effective daily rate being better during some periods than others.

The limit to conversion periods

So, if you make more compound interest the more conversion periods there are in a year, is there any limit to the amount of interest you can earn as the number of conversion periods per year increases? Pure maths says that there is, and gives the term:

$$e^i - 1$$

where e = 2.71828 and i = the interest rate. $e^i - 1$ tells you the total interest you will get in a year 'in the limit' where you have conversion periods at every moment in time. Thus, if the interest rate is 10%, the maximum interest you can earn, however many conversion periods there are in a year, is:

$$2.71828^{0.1} - 1 = 10.52\%$$

e is always 2.71828, a curious number which, when used as the base for logarithms (see page 200), simplifies some general formulae.

To illustrate this, consider the growth rate of the beanstalks in the fairy tale 'Jack and the Beanstalk'. The beanstalks grow rapidly, and their growth rate is continuous. Assume they approximately double their size every day. If you checked them after half a day, they would have grown about 1.5 times, and if you checked them after quarter of a day they would have grown about 1.25 times. As in compound interest, the effective daily growth rate increases the more conversion periods you have, but as the number of conversion periods becomes very large and the conversion periods become shorter and shorter, you approach continuous growth (as occurs for real beanstalks) which, even for the most energetic beanstalk, is limited in rate.

Comparing different conversion periods

If you are comparing several investments with different conversion periods, you need to convert them all to the same period, which is usually taken as being the rate with one conversion period (i.e. paying the interest once a year only). This is called the 'effective interest rate'. To work it out, use the formula:

$$i = [1 + (I \div k)]^k - 1$$

where i is the rate of interest as a proportion of the sum invested, I is the effective interest rate and k is the number of conversion periods in the year.

Example

Calculate the effective interest rate of an investment of £1,000 at 10% with two conversion periods:

$$\text{Effective rate} = [1 + (0.1 \div 2)]^2 - 1$$
$$= [1 + (0.05)]^2 - 1$$
$$= 1.05^2 - 1$$
$$= 0.1025$$

The effective rate is 10.25%

Now that we are working with general formulae, let's consider ones for future value and present value and compound interest.

Future value and present value formulae

Earlier we saw that the future value (FV) of an investment is the total of the sum invested plus all the interest you will get during the time you invest, and that present value (PV) means the sum you are investing.

Say, the PV is 1,000 and the interest rate is 10% with four conversion periods per year. To calculate the PV in five years, use the formula:

$$FV = PV \times [1 + (i \div k)]^{k \times n}$$

where i is the rate of interest per annum as a proportion of the sum invested (e.g. 10% = 0.1), k is the number of conversion periods in a year and n is the number of years.

$$FV = 1,000 \times [1 + (0.1 \div 4)]^{4 \times 5}$$
$$= 1,000 \times (1 + 0.025)^{20}$$
$$= 1,000 \times 1.025^{20}$$
$$= 1,000 \times 1.63859$$
$$= 1,638.59$$

So, £1,000 invested at 10% compound interest for five years with four conversion periods a year will give a total (future value) of £1,638.59.

If you know the future value but not the present value, you can rearrange the formula to find it:

$$PV = FV \div [1 + (i \div k)]^{k \times n}$$

If you know that the FV is £1,638.59 after five years at 10% with four conversion periods per year:

$$PV = 1,638.59 \div [1 + (0.1 \div 4)]^{4 \times 5}$$
$$= 1,638.59 \div (1 + 0.025)^{20}$$
$$= 1,638.59 \div 1.025^{20}$$
$$= 1,638.59 \div 1,638.59$$
$$= 1,000$$

Notice that even though you don't know what the PV is, you still know what i is because you know the percentage of it you're getting as interest per annum (10% = one tenth = 0.1). You can also calculate the compound interest (CI) as FV − PV. In this example,

$$CI = 1,638.59 - 1,000 = 638.59.$$

Discounting the principal

When money is lent for a specified period, the interest is sometimes taken off the principal (the sum lent or invested) at the beginning. A bank might lend you £100,000 at 10% and only give you £90,000 of it, keeping the other £10,000 as the interest.

In the UK, this also happens in the money markets where 'bills of exchange' (a kind of IOU) are bought and sold at discount instead of at a rate of interest. Suppose a bill of exchange for £1 million is due to be settled in three months' time. It might be sold for 98% of £1 million, giving the buyer a profit of 2% of £1 million in return for waiting for three months to get the money back, which is equivalent to getting interest on the money.

Discounting interest on consumer loans causes confusion in the minds of the borrowers: someone who borrows £1,000 at 10% interest p.a. discounted and repayable over a year may think that the total interest payable will be 10% p.a., but it will actually be considerably more.

As we've seen, there are traps for the unwary in the comparison of interest rates. £1,000 at 10% interest a year with 12 conversion periods gives 10.47% interest (the effective rate), while two conversion periods would only produce a 10.25% effective rate, so the former is the better rate.

Lenders have profited from the public's lack of awareness of this phenomenon, so laws have been introduced in many countries to help consumers compare rates more easily. In the US, the law says that the effective rate must always be stated. In the UK, interest rates must usually be given in two forms, a rate of the advertiser's choice, such as the 'flat rate', which calculates interest on the whole sum lent even after part of it has been repaid, and the APR, or annual percentage rate, which adds hidden extras such as commissions, charges for documents and maintenance to the effective rate. The APRs on credit cards, for instance, are often quite a shock when compared with the other rate quoted.

7

The stock markets: some theories and techniques

The world's financial markets have developed greatly in their complexity during the last three decades, but can still be divided into a few basic types:

- The currency markets, for foreign exchange.
- The money markets, for short-term lending (usually less than 1 year).
- The bond markets, for long-term borrowing by governments and large firms.
- The equity markets; 'equities' are shares in companies that are bought and sold by investors.
- The derivatives markets, for complex securities 'derived' from an underlying asset, such as bonds, shares or physical commodities.

The term 'stock market' is generally used to refer to the equity markets, or sometimes more generally to all the financial markets. In this chapter 'stock market' will be used to mean just the equity markets. The financial markets are interrelated, and many of the larger players, such as governments, large corporations, and financial institutions, such as banks and pension funds, participate in all of them simultaneously, as investors, borrowers and providers of services. Each type of market has a distinct function that can be understood as essentially useful; the fact that it is possible to win or lose large sums through speculation in the markets is a separate issue.

The unique function of the stock market is that it allows people and organisations that possess money to acquire part ownership, through purchasing shares, in companies that are striving to build value through productive activities. In the main stock markets most shares can be bought and sold at the market price at any time during business hours, providing investors with good liquidity (they can convert their shares to cash quickly) and overall, shares have produced better average returns than all other financial assets in the long term. Thus the main benefit to investors is the chance of obtaining better returns in the long term while retaining the ability to sell some or all of their shares at any time. From the companies' point of view, the main benefit of issuing shares on the stock market is the ability to raise large sums of risk capital that do not have to be repaid (unlike a loan), which can in the right conditions allow a company to grow much faster than it could otherwise. Overall, the stock market can be said to have a useful social and economic function in that it provides savers (people and organisations with money) with a highly efficient way of putting their capital into the most productive kind of investments (successful companies). The stock market is not, of course, the only system ever invented for moving capital around the economy – think of the heavily centralised state-owned economy in the USSR – but it may well be the most effective system, in spite of its volatility and vulnerability to crises.

The aim of this chapter to examine what is understood theoretically about how the stock market system works, and to dispel some of the common misapprehensions (held even by many market professionals). Mathematically speaking, the stock market is, as yet, full of unsolved problems. Because of the allure of potentially huge short-term profits, many attempts have been made to predict the market, but none have been very successful in the long term. In this chapter we will review some of these theories and examine ways in which they are unsatisfactory. Much of the mathematics is too complicated to be dealt with in this book, but we will be able to cover some of the basic calculations.

What does winning in the stock market mean?

Before we look at some of the techniques and theories used by market players, it's worth considering a few general points. First, most of the people and organisations that have made large fortunes in the stock market have not done so principally by buying shares in the market, selling them later at a profit, and repeating the process. More often, they amass riches by.

- charging large fees for financial services;
- owning a large part of a private firm that is later 'floated' on the stock market, allowing them to sell their shares for a very big profit; or
- serving in a senior position in a large company and receiving generous options to buy the company's own shares and other lucrative deals.

In other words, they have special opportunities to make large profits that are not available to the majority of investors. Two of the world's most famous investors, Warren Buffett and George Soros, have very different philosophical approaches to stock market investment, but in both cases the bulk of their fortunes were made in ways that were simply not open to outsiders. Buffett started as a manager of an investment fund for other investors, but used his extraordinary skills to acquire controlling interests in businesses. Unlike most investors, who passively buy and sell shares in companies over which they have no influence, he has been actively involved as a business owner for many decades. George Soros, a Hungarian émigré to America, had his first long run of success in the 1960s managing what would now be called a hedge fund. He specialised in making educated guesses about the economic effects of political decisions in Europe, then still recovering from the economic damage of World War Two, at a time when most Wall Street professionals knew nothing of the world outside the US and when European governments were financially unsophisticated.

Buffett and Soros are widely recognised as having unusual talents and may well deserve their success, but even if the returns from investing in shares were the result of pure chance, there would still be a few outstanding winners. One of the problems of investment is how to assess whether or not unusually good returns from a particular investment approach is the result of chance. Probability (see Chapter 8) tells us that in the short term there will be quite a few outstanding winners in the market; the real test of an investment method is whether an investor can perform outstandingly well over many decades.

Furthermore, it is always possible for the unscrupulous to try to look as though they are winners even when their performance is mediocre. We all hear the stories and meet the people: they can't do anything wrong, they always make money, they have the Midas touch. Naturally we want to know what they've got that we don't. How is it that they have become winners? We should be aware that it may simply be a function of probability; in any race, someone has to win.

Suppose you eat out regularly with a colleague for many years, and always flip a coin at the end of the meal to see who will pay. After you've done it thousands of times, one of you is going to be seriously out of pocket, despite the fact that overall, the ratio of heads to tails gets closer and closer to 1:1 the more often you do it. This is because the monetary value of the difference between your wins and your colleague's wins is likely to be greater the more you play, even if the difference itself is getting smaller as a proportion of the total cost of all the meals. In addition, the person who gets ahead is quite likely to stay ahead for a very long time. It might take a lifetime for the lead to swap to the other person. Thus, if you've played the game for 10 years, the winner at the end is quite likely to have been ahead 90% of the time. Is this person a winner who has special knowledge, or a magic touch? Obviously not; the winner is simply benefiting from chance. In the stock market, there may be individuals who are highly successful simply because of random events; no special significance should be attached to their success.

Deceit in prediction

Here's an illegal confidence trick that illustrates the need for scepticism in following the advice of a successful predictor. Suppose you are an investment adviser, and you write to 100,000 investors predicting the change in the value of a stock index. You tell 50,000 investors that the value will rise in a month, and the other 50,000 that it will fall. A month later, you write to the 50,000 who received the correct prediction, making a further prediction, again telling 25,000 the value will rise and the other 25,000 that it will fall. In the third month you have 25,000 people to whom you have made two correct predictions. Apply the same technique three more times, and you will have 3,250 people to whom you have given five correct predictions. Now you write to them asking for money, say £800, to continue sending them your information which has 'proven' its value. If half of them pay up, you've just made £1,300,000. Naturally, you will have supported your predictions with spurious claims about the techniques and theories you have employed. It is now time to disappear with the loot before you are caught.

Approaches to stock market investment

Let's examine some of the techniques that are really used by stock market investors. Many of them are based on contradictory theories, and a few may simply be false, but they have all been used to invest large sums in the markets.

The Kondratiev wave

Nikolai Kondratiev was a brilliant young Russian economist in the early twentieth century who gave his name to this cycle. Western economists became interested in his work after he successfully predicted the depression of the 1930s and the subsequent boom. His ideas cost him his life: he died in a Stalinist labour camp in the late 1930s.

Also known as the 'long wave', it is, on the face of it, an implausible idea: that there are recurring long-term cycles of boom and slump in the world economy (see Figure 7.1). It has at times been an unpopular idea, because it is so directly opposed to the grand vision of an ever-growing world economy upon which so much policy has been based, but periodically it has been taken very seriously, for example by the influential economist Joseph Schumpeter, and the eminent historian Eric Hobsbawm. The long wave is said to take between 45 and 60 years to go from peak to peak, but interpretations of the timing of previous waves vary very widely indeed.

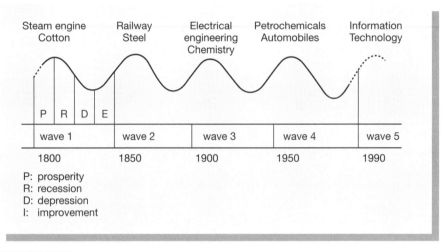

Figure 7.1   Schematic diagram of the long wave

Although the theory has some intellectual respectability as a hypothesis, it also attracts a great many enthusiasts who use it as a rhetorical technique to support their own wild predictions about the future of the stock market, the economy and society in general. The existence of the long wave has not been proved. It is difficult to prove that any economic cycle exists without showing that it has repeated itself many times; if you go back four long waves (say, 200 years) from the present, you get to the beginning of the Industrial Revolution, which is arguably the starting point of modern economies. Four waves is too small a sample, many would argue, to prove the existence of a cycle. Another difficulty is the lack of trustworthy data before about 1870: many long-wave enthusiasts are really just making things up when they provide detailed illustrations of the stages of past waves.

More than one explanation has been offered for how the long wave might work. Briefly, Kondratiev himself thought that during the upswing industrial economies expanded as fast as they could until the primary producing countries were unable to keep up with the demand for raw materials. The downswing then began, driving capital and labour abroad to 'new' countries (e.g. Australia and America), and stimulating inventions and discoveries which would be exploited in the next upswing as the new countries increased their supply of raw materials.

The long wave is perhaps a useful way of exploring and interpreting the extraordinary processes of modernisation that have been transforming the world for the last two centuries, but there is no convincing evidence that it can be used to make precise forecasts, especially not in the short term. For most stock market investors, the short term and the medium term are the most important time periods because, as the famous economist J.M. Keynes once said, 'in the long term we are all dead'. In other words, investors prefer to make profits sooner rather than later if they possibly can.

Technical analysis

'Technical analysis' is an umbrella term for a collection of investment methods that seek to predict the movements of share prices in the short term. If you go to the stock market section of any large bookshop, you will find that it is mainly dominated by two types of books: first, a lot of dumbed-down, get-rich-quick books, like the bizarrely imbecilic *Rich Dad, Poor Dad* by Robert Kiyosaki, and second, a range of serious-looking books about technical analysis, containing a lot of impressive charts and diagrams. Confronted by these volumes, a non-specialist would easily assume that technical analysis is an intellectually respectable discipline based on a great body of supporting evidence. In reality, the evidence that any of the techniques of technical analysis can be used to make profits consistently is surprisingly thin, even though it has been used in stock market investing for more than a century.

Technical analysts, some of whom are called 'chartists', try to predict future stock trends by analysing past movements. The purists don't ever look at any other information, such as political events or industrial data; they concentrate on studying the changes in stock values alone, believing that it is unnecessary to know why the changes have occurred.

Technical analysis makes three main assumptions:

1 That patterns identified in charts of share price movements recur.

2 That share price movements have predictable trends.

3 That all the factors that influence stock prices are immediately reflected in the price and so do not need to be considered separately.

Patterns in charts

Figure 7.2 shows an example of one of the best known patterns used by technical analysts, called the 'head and shoulders reversal pattern'. Points A and F are called the 'left and right shoulders', respectively, points B and D the 'neckline', and point C is called the 'head'. The idea is that if you see a head and shoulders pattern forming, prices have reached a 'top' and will start declining.

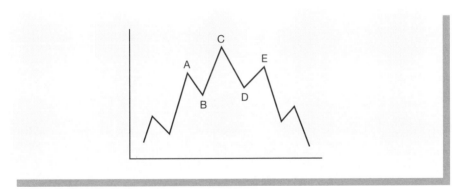

Figure 7.2   The head and shoulders pattern

Figure 7.3 shows a 'flag'. This is supposed to be a reliable sign that an upward price trend will continue. There are many other patterns recognised by technical analysts, and each analyst seems to have their own particular favourites. Many technical analysts believe that it is the psychology of investors en masse that are the cause of these patterns. One of the main problems of this approach, however, is that it is highly subjective. Technical analysts rarely agree on how to interpret the data in a chart, and often explain away inaccurate forecasts by saying that they did not interpret the chart properly. But unless a technique can be explained clearly enough for someone else to reproduce it and obtain the same results (this is one of the main tests for the validity of scientific experiments), there is no

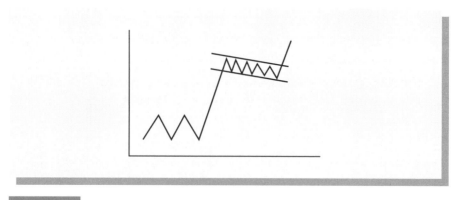

Figure 7.3   A flag

way of knowing what the technique really is or whether it works. Simply saying after an incorrect prediction that you failed to interpret a chart properly, without being able to explain, before making the prediction, all the rules you are using to interpret the data, makes it impossible to test whether your method of interpretation works or not.

The Dow theory

Charles Dow published the first stock market average in 1884 and was the father of technical analysis. His theory is based on the following principles:

1   There are three kinds of trends in the market: primary, secondary and minor. To explain them, Dow used the simile of the movements of the sea: a primary trend is like the tide, a secondary trend is like the waves in the tide and a minor trend is like the ripples on the waves.

2   There are three phases to major trends. Dow said that there is an 'accumulation phase', when the smart money spots the right moment to buy, a second phase when the technical analysts jump on the band wagon and a final 'distributive' phase when the public starts buying as the news gets out, and the smart money starts selling, or 'distributing'.

3   All the averages and indices – in Dow's time, this simply meant the Industrial and Rail averages in the US – must confirm each other for a trend to exist.

4   A trend continues until signals (the patterns that technical analysts think are important) appear in the charts that it has reversed.

There are lots of other versions and theories of technical analysis. These days, the 'Elliott wave' is more often used than the Dow theory.

The Elliott wave

The Elliott wave theory was invented by an American accountant named Ralph Elliott who, like all good technical analysts, believed that you could spot recurring patterns in the stock market. Figure 7.4 shows a schematic Elliott wave.

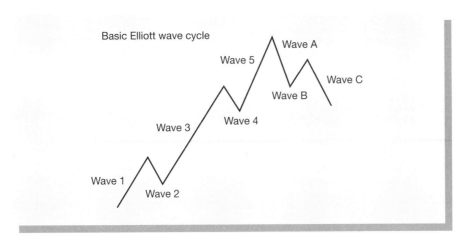

Basic Elliott wave cycle

Wave A
Wave 5
Wave C
Wave B
Wave 4
Wave 3
Wave 1
Wave 2

Figure 7.4   **The Elliott wave**

The idea is that the stock market has a 'supercycle', which is rather like the Kondratiev wave. There are two and a half cycles on the way up, followed by one and half on the way down. The same pattern is supposed to exist in smaller portions of time, such as annually, monthly, daily and minute by minute. In his later years, Elliott began to claim that this pattern existed in all parts of nature, on all scales, from the cosmic to the subatomic, a very ancient idea that was used in many pre-scientific predictive arts, such as astrology.

Is there any evidence that technical analysis can be used to predict share price movements?

As technical analysis covers a very wide range of different techniques, many of which are not clearly defined, it is very difficult to test them. Much of the academic research that has been done on it uses 'backtesting', which simply means testing how a method would have performed during a given period in the past. This is better than nothing, but it does not tell you how the method will perform in the future, when conditions may have changed. There is some research that suggests that a handful of technical analysis techniques have worked during some periods in the past – but this is very far from establishing that a given technique is always successful.

Private investors must use brokers to buy and sell, and brokers take a commission for each transaction. Technical analysis encourages frequent trading, because you are supposed to respond to the 'buy' and 'sell' signals indicated in the charts in order to make your money. This means that your brokerage charges are going to be far higher than those of a long-term investor who holds on to shares for years. For a technical analysis strategy to be worthwhile, it must therefore produce better results than simply holding a portfolio of shares for a long time, to compensate for the increased transaction costs.

Private investors need to reflect on the fact that it is in a broker's interest to have clients trade frequently, and that a client who believes in technical analysis is going to make the broker more money in commissions than one who rarely buys and sells. So just because many financial institutions have teams of technical analysts who provide advice to their clients based on predicting chart patterns, it doesn't necessarily follow that technical analysis works; it may just be a good way of getting more business from certain types of customers.

Incidentally, when brokers persuade clients to switch investments unnecessarily in order to earn more fees, it is known as 'churning', which is illegal in many stock markets. The trouble is that it is often very difficult to prove what 'unnecessarily' really means. Trying to spot patterns in charts is strangely attractive to many obsessive-compulsive types, and as long as they themselves are certain that there is some hidden truth within technical analysis that they will eventually uncover, and they are willing to risk their capital on frequent trading, who is the broker to stop them? It should also be said that technical analysis enthusiasts are not the only people who are vulnerable to 'churning' – it's a common problem in broker–customer relationships.

Batteries of mathematical tests on a century of stock prices in London and New York seem to have shown that such correlations as exist between past and future prices are too small to beat trading costs; there is no evidence to support the idea that trends in stock movements are other than random, except for an overall long-term trend of growth across the entire market. Randomly selecting stocks and holding them produces results which are just as good, if not better. Flipping a coin many times will produce long runs of just heads or just tails, and when plotted on a chart will produce patterns of the kind that technical analysts like; however, we know from probability theory (see Chapter 8) that each flip of the coin is independent of the previous flips, and that long runs are simply chance, not trends.

Nevertheless, large banks and other financial institutions continue to pay large salaries to technical analysts, some of whom presumably do make good predictions. The point about this phenomenon is that, from a mathematical point of view, success does not in itself prove anything. A Cambridge mathematics professor says, 'There are traders who may be successful due to intuition and specialised knowledge who honestly ascribe their success to a baseless technique.' In other words, it is very human to try to explain good results, but the explanation may simply be wrong.

Alternatively, it may be that if there are enough technical analysts engaged in advisory positions, they somehow unintentionally combine together to produce a self-fulfilling prophecy. Things can't be quite as simple as this, however, as there is another group of analysts, the 'counter-cyclical analysts', who believe that the best strategy is to do exactly the opposite of what technical analysts and others are recommending. This view is called 'contrarian'.

So, if we don't believe in technical analysis, is there any other way to make money from the market in the short term? The theory of fundamental analysis says that there is.

Fundamental analysis

Fundamental analysts attempt to predict future prices by finding out what a share is really worth: its 'intrinsic value'. This may have little to do with its current market price. Unlike technical analysis, which often relies on nebulous, quasi-mystical ideas about patterns in investment behaviour and tends to ignore any information about the companies themselves, fundamental analysis tries to take a rational approach to understanding the businesses of the companies whose shares are traded in the market. In other words, the idea is to understand what is going on in a real business, and then make a judgement about the future prospects of that company.

First, the prospects for the industry as a whole are examined, and then the records, plans and management of individual companies within the industry are subjected to a thorough scrutiny. An estimate of the company's future earnings is then made, incorporating estimates of future sales, overheads, accounting policies and a host of other factors that might affect profit. Broadly speaking, stock market professionals tend to have a lot more faith in fundamental analysis than technical analysis, because it deals with the nuts and bolts of real companies. Professional fundamental analysts, so the argument goes, will achieve better returns than the small investor because they are better informed.

In Chapter 6 we looked at discounted cash flow (DCF), which is perhaps the best tool of fundamental analysis, and is widely used by stock market professionals. As we saw, however, for all its complex calculations and reliance on real data, DCF is still based on subjective judgements and assumptions. Furthermore, the business performance of a company in the real world is not always very closely tied to the fluctuations in its share price; it is not, perhaps, unreasonable to hope that solid profit growth, for instance, will eventually lead to a higher share price, but it may take a surprisingly long time to happen. Conversely, the dodgiest, most fly-by-night firm may enjoy huge popularity among investors and a rocketing share price for an extended period, even though fundamental analysis shows that something is very wrong with its underlying business.

In this respect the stock market can be a bit like betting on a beauty competition, where you try to bet on the competitor who you think the majority will think is the most beautiful, and not on the competitor who you yourself think is the most beautiful. As soon as you begin to do this, you start to abandon your study of the 'fundamental' aspects of the underlying businesses, and instead focus on comparative measures. Comparisons present many difficult problems, which can be illustrated using the best known comparative measure, the Price/Earnings ratio.

The comparative approach: the Price/Earnings ratio (PE)

Let's suppose that an analyst has carefully estimated what a particular company will earn in the future, using expert judgement and large amounts of business information. What next? Often the analyst then turns to comparisons, looking at the company's current share price, calculating the ratio of price to earnings (PE) and then comparing the PE with that of other firms.

If you look at the stock market pages of the *Financial Times*, you will find that the PE ratio is listed for you. If the PE is six, it means that the price of the share is six times the share's proportion of the annual profit stated in the most recently published accounts of the company.

Thus:

$$\text{PE ratio} = \text{price per share} \div \text{earnings per share}$$

So if the earnings per share is 9p and the share price is 180p, the PE is:

$$\text{PE} = 180 \div 9 = 20$$

Notice that this is equivalent to the earnings being 5% of the share price. This implies that if the company's earnings remained steady, it would take 20 years for it to generate profits equivalent to its current market price (this is like the payback concept we saw in Chapter 6).

A large, well-established company may have a fairly low PE ratio, say 10, because it is thought that its prospects for growth are low, while a small company in a high technology industry may have a very high PE, say 40 or more, because it is thought likely that its earnings will sky-rocket in a few years' time. PE ratios are also affected greatly by external factors such as recessions, when they tend to go up in anticipation that a recovery will increase future earnings.

When interest rates are high, an investor can make a high return by keeping money in safe, stable bonds and other interest-bearing instruments outside the market. Fundamentalists, therefore, compare interest rates with returns from stocks. Low interest rates are seen to make the market more attractive because of its potential for higher returns, so when interest rates are low, the 'intrinsic value' of stocks is thought to be higher.

As with all ratios, there are variations in the way that PE can be defined. The definition we have just used is the most common one, and is called the 'current PE'. A similar measure is the 'trailing PE', which instead of using the earnings from the most recent annual accounts, uses an average of the earnings over the last four three-month periods. Another PE you are likely to encounter is the 'forward PE', which is based on estimates of future earnings over the coming 12 months. Often this figure is given without telling us where these estimates have come from, which is unhelpful. Furthermore, although 'price per share' usually means the current market price of the share, some analysts choose to take any average of the price over a recent period. Also, earnings per share should be adjusted for options to buy shares, bonds that are convertible to shares, and other obscure instruments that the company may have issued.

All these different ways of calculating PEs can give surprisingly different results, so it is very important for analysts to know how the PEs they are using have been calculated, and to make sure they are properly comparable.

Comparisons can be problematic for other reasons too. For example, if the analyst takes the mean average PE of a group of companies – let's say, mobile phone manufacturers – the group may contain some companies that have unusually low earnings, which will push up their PEs, and the mean PE. In this case, it would be better to use a median PE. Alternatively, some firms in the group might have no earnings, which makes it impossible to calculate the PE. If they are excluded, it will bias the PE towards the more profitable firms.

Analysts often aren't in a position to calculate all the PEs themselves, especially when they are trying to compare whole industries across the world, or the PEs of different countries' stock markets. PEs vary enormously between countries, and are not a good guide to 'intrinsic' value. Countries with high expected growth rates are likely to have higher PEs because investors are willing to pay a high price for shares in companies that have a higher earnings growth rate. Markets with high interest rates are likely to have lower PEs because the reciprocal of the PE is the rate of return an investor expects – for example, a PE of 10 is similar to an interest rate of 10% and a PE of 5 is similar to an interest rate of 20%.

Table 7.1 PE ratios around the world in 2009

Country	Index	PE
China	Shanghai Comp	19.24
Russia	Russian Trading	8
US	S&P 500	10.21
UK	FTSE100	14.11
Japan	Nikkei 225	34.01

When comparing firms within an industry, it is important to recognise that industry classifications can be very arbitrary, because many firms are changing their activities so much. Different firms in the same industry may have very different growth rates, risks and businesses, and so may be difficult to compare.

Does fundamental analysis work?

Fundamentalists believe that past earnings can be a good indicator of future growth; if the management of a company is very good, so the thinking goes, then it will continue to be good in the future. Five years is a long time in the stock market, and most fundamental analysts hope to make good predictions for shorter periods than this.

Many studies have shown, however, that the analysts' predictions show massive errors and are, if anything, worse for short-term predictions than for five-yearly ones. Two reasons why this may be so are randomness and the variety of different accounting methods in use. The effects of random events in the real world, such as natural disasters and political events, can throw out the most sound estimates of a company's future earnings for obvious reasons; as yet there is no way of predicting them. Accounting methods (particularly the so-called 'creative' accounting methods) can distort profits hugely: the special accounting methods for depreciation, land, leasing, insurance and conglomerates, to name but a few, can confuse even the most sharp-eyed analyst.

So, if the theories used by market professionals aren't very sound, how does the market really work? In the 1960s, academics developed the idea that there was absolutely no way to beat the market other than by getting information more quickly than anyone else. Since all the thousands of highly competitive analysts obtained the same information at the same time, they argue, prices would immediately reflect any new information and the market must be 'efficient' (see Chapter 7).

Risk

It has been argued that risk is the only characteristic of a stock that is worth measuring. One way of defining risk is to say that it is the risk that you will not obtain the return on your investment that you would expect, as estimated by the method described below.

Suppose you can get a guaranteed 'risk-free' return of 5% a year by investing in government bonds:

One-year government bond 5%

Your expected return = 5%, because that is what the government has guaranteed to pay you.

Your actual return = 5%, because that is what the government does pay you.

As we saw in Chapter 6, nothing is completely risk-free, but we accept that US and UK government bonds are as close as you can get. Knowing that you can obtain 5% from a risk-free bond, why would you bother to invest in shares, which are known to be riskier as an asset class? The only reason to do so is if you believe that you have a chance of achieving a return that is substantially higher than 5%.

Suppose you buy some shares, hold them for a year, and then sell them. It is likely that your actual return is different from your expected return (see below for how this is calculated). Figure 7.5 shows how a hypothetical 'variance' between the expected return and the actual return might be distributed.

The distribution in Figure 7.5 has positive skew, so in this case the chance of achieving a better actual return that the expected return is higher than the chance of achieving a worse actual return.

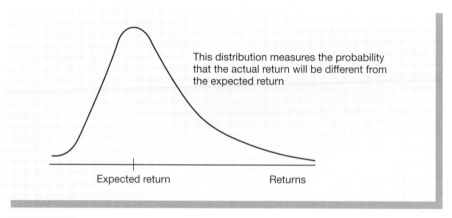

Figure 7.5   A variance distribution

Figure 7.6 shows two hypothetical variances for two different investments, one with high variance and the other with low variance.

Shares with low variance might be of a large, well-established company that has dependable businesses that produce few surprises. Shares with high variance might be of a smaller company that is entering new, exciting markets but encounters many setbacks and experiences large swings in its profits and share price over time. The 'riskier' share is the one with the higher variance: it is riskier in the sense that we don't know if it will do much better or much worse than the expected return.

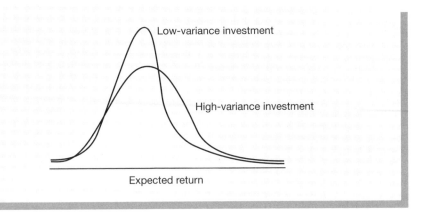

Figure 7.6   **High variance versus low variance investment**

Measuring a risk means we can give it a value, and a popular way to measure risk is to calculate it as the variance, or the standard deviation, of the returns.

Example

Imagine you are analysing a stock which has existed for 21 years. For seven of those years it has produced an 8% return, in seven years it has produced a 24% return, and in seven years it has produced an 8% loss.

Calculating the variance, we get:

$$\text{The average} = (24 + 8 - 8) \div 3 = 8$$

The average is also known as the 'expected return'.

$$\begin{aligned}\text{Variance} &= \{(24 - 8)^2 + (8 - 8)^2 + (-8 - 8)^2\} \div 3 \\ &= (16 + 0 + 16) \div 3 \\ &= (256 + 256) \div 3 \\ &= 170.67\end{aligned}$$

$$\text{Standard deviation} = \sqrt{\text{variance}} = \sqrt{170.67} = 13.06$$

If we go on to calculate the variance or standard deviation of other shares and find that they are larger, we can say that they are more risky, meaning that in the past they have been more volatile.

US studies of the performance of large numbers of shares and bonds confirm this approach. The dispersion of returns for common stocks and small company stocks is far wider than for bonds and US Treasury bills, indicating that stocks are more volatile, or risky. The average annual rate of return for shares has been far higher, and has far outpaced inflation, represented by the consumer price index (CPI). This evidence tends to confirm the idea that you get what you pay for in terms of risk. Shares are more risky than bonds but produce a higher rate of return over the long term. An investor who is prepared to buy and hold a diverse collection of shares for several decades is likely to do better than one who holds bonds.

Investors often try to spread their risk by investing in a number of shares (a portfolio), hoping that while some of the shares may go down, others will go up, and that overall they will obtain an acceptable return. One common way of doing this is to invest in a professionally managed fund. There is a great variety of funds to choose from. In general, a fund describes its overall strategies and goals to investors, and provides benchmarks – often stock market indices or other, similar funds – against which investors can measure the fund's performance. The idea is that investors who want stability in the value of their assets can choose a balanced fund, which invests in a mixture of shares and bonds (bonds are much less volatile than shares), investors who want growth can invest in a fund that backs potentially high growth companies (this is likely to produce very volatile returns) and investors who would be satisfied with the returns produced by a stock market index, such as the FTSE100, can invest in an index-tracker fund which mimics the components and weighting of the index.

Modern Portfolio Theory (MPT)

Modern Portfolio Theory, which isn't so modern anymore and has been superseded by other theories to some extent, assumes that investors want the least possible risk for a given return, and offers a way of investing in a portfolio of shares that is less risky than investing in any of the particular stocks within it.

Imagine you are investing in a tiny country that has only two industries and two seasons. It has an alpine resort and a beach club. When the weather is good, the beach club does well, and when the weather is bad, the alpine resort booms. The returns for the two resorts are shown in Table 7.2.

Table 7.2 Returns for two resorts

	Alpine resort	*Beach club*
Good weather	–30%	60%
Bad weather	60%	–30%

If the probability of a particular season having good or bad weather is one in two, investing in the alpine resort would produce returns of 60% half the time, and –30% half the time, giving an average, or expected return, of 15%; the same is true for investing in the beach club. It would be risky, though, to invest in only one of the resorts because there might be many seasons one after the other with the same weather, just as you might get a long row of heads when flipping a coin.

If you invested £100 in each of the resorts, your results over five seasons might be as shown in Table 7.3.

Table 7.3 Investment results (£100 in each of two resorts over five seasons)

Season	Alpine resort	Beach club	
Good	–30	60	
Bad	60	–30	
Bad	60	–30	
Bad	60	–30	
Bad	60	–30	
Total	210	–60	= 150

You have lost £60 on the beach club, but made £210 on the alpine resort, giving you an overall return on your £200 investment of £150.

If you had invested all of your £200 in the alpine resort, you would have made £420. If you had invested the whole £200 in the beach club you would have lost £120 of your capital, leaving you with only £80 to reinvest. It would take time to get your money back to its original level and, if you attempted to do so by investing again in only one of the two resorts, you might well make a further substantial loss. Thus, the argument for spreading the risk is very strong.

The two resorts have negative covariance. Here is the formula for calculating covariance. Let Ag and AB be the actual returns from the alpine resort in good and bad weather respectively, and $\bar{A}$ be the expected return (average), Bg and BB be the actual returns from the beach club, and $\bar{B}$ the expected return:

$$\text{The covariance between A and B} = \text{COV(AB)} =$$
$$\text{prob. of good weather } (Ag - \bar{A})(Bg - \bar{B}) + \text{prob. of bad}$$
$$\text{weather } (AB - \bar{A})(BB - \bar{B})$$

In our example, the probability of good or bad weather are both 0.5, so:

$$\text{COV(AB)} = [0.5(-30 - 15)(60 - 15) + 0.5(60 - 15)(-30 - 15)]$$
$$= 0.5(-45 \times 45) + 0.5(45 \times -45)$$
$$= -0.10125 + -0.10125$$
$$= -0.2025$$

In real life, however, many shares tend not to have negative covariance, but instead often move up and down together, so it is rare to find a perfect opportunity to eliminate risk. It is possible, though, to reduce risk by investing in shares with a low covariance or, better still, a negative covariance. This is called diversification, and can be achieved by investing across a wide number of industries and countries; private investors can do this through investment funds.

The Capital Asset Pricing Model (CAPM)

Like MPT, Capital Asset Pricing Model has had its day, but it still has its devotees. It is based on the idea that the variability of the stock market as a whole, known as market risk, is different from the variability of individual shares. Fundamental analysis may discover influences on a particular company that cause it to rise or fall, such as labour problems or a new patent, but all shares tend to rise and fall with the market overall. The market risk prevents investors from being able to completely eliminate their risk of making a loss by diversifying in companies with negative covariance. In our example of the tiny country, we could think of the market risk as being the possibility of, say, fewer tourists coming to the country because of economic or political problems elsewhere. Fewer tourists would reduce the profit potential for both resorts, whatever the season.

To compare the movements of a particular share against the market overall, we say that the 'beta' (the Greek letter 'b', written β) of the market risk is 1. A share with a beta of 3 will swing three times as much as the market does in either direction, and a share with a beta of 1.5 will swing only one and a half times as far. Thus, the higher the beta of a portfolio or individual share, the more risky it is.

Diversifying cannot reduce the investor's exposure to the overall market risk, but what it can do is bring the risk of a portfolio down to a beta of 1, the same as the market risk beta. This idea can be extended to valuing stocks in terms of the total risk. CAPM says that it is only the overall market risk that is relevant for valuation of a stock, since the part of the risk that is peculiar to an individual stock, the 'unsystematic risk', can be eliminated by diversification, just as we did on our hypothetical country. As a rule of thumb, CAPM says that a portfolio of as few as 20 diversified stocks should be enough to eliminate almost all of the unsystematic risk.

Giving the overall market risk a beta value of 1, and a risk-free investment, such as a bank deposit, a beta value of 0, CAPM uses the following formula to work out the expected return on a diversified portfolio:

Expected return on a share = Risk-free interest rate + [Beta of the share × (Expected return on the market − Risk-free interest rate)]

The reason for calculating the expected return is that CAPM states that if, in the long term, you want to get a higher rate of return than the market average, all you have to do is to increase the beta value of your portfolio.

Example

You have £100,000 to invest and you decide to work out the expected return from four choices:

1 a risk-free investment in a bank deposit;

2 an investment of half your money in the stock market and the other half risk-free;

3 investing the whole sum in a portfolio with a beta in line with that of the market average;

4 a high-risk portfolio.

You find that you can get 5% interest from the bank deposit, and that the market average return is 8% per annum.

Choice 1

Your expected return is the interest rate the bank gives you: 5%, or £5,000.

Choice 2

You decide to put £50,000 in a portfolio with a beta of 1, and the rest in a bank. Using the expected return formula,

The expected rate of return = 5% + 0.5(8% − 5%) = 6.5%.

Note that although the portfolio has a beta of 1, you have only invested 50% of your money, so you must halve the beta value.

Choice 3

You invest all the money in a portfolio with a beta of 1; your expected rate of return will therefore be in line with the market average, 8%.

Choice 4

You invest in a portfolio with a beta of 2.5, which should generate higher returns; expected rate of return = 5% + 2.5(8% − 5%) = 12.5%.

Beta is an officially approved way of measuring risk, and you can obtain estimates of the beta of a stock from brokers and investment advisers.

Criticisms of CAPM

A portfolio with a beta of 0 should, according to CAPM, produce the same return as a risk-free investment outside the market which also, by definition, has a beta of 0 too. Studies have shown, however, that over the long term stock portfolios with a beta of 0 have done better than risk-free investments, contradicting the theory. In addition, in the 1980s mutual funds in the US produced returns that had no correlation to their beta values. There have been objections to the way that beta values are measured, and it has been shown that betas for individual shares fluctuate significantly over time.

Perhaps the most serious criticism of CAPM, though, is the argument that none of the market indices are a perfect reflection of the overall market risk; in fact, calculating beta using different indices have produced widely differing beta values for stocks. It has been said that you cannot measure the overall market risk accurately; if this is so, then CAPM is untestable, and therefore useless. Many investors do continue to use CAPM, however.

Arbitrage Pricing Theory (APT)

Like CAPM, APT says that it is the overall market risk element of the total risk of a stock that should be measured. To do this, a number of risk factors have been identified to be used in addition to beta. These include inflation rates, interest rates, company size and price–earnings ratios.

We should also look briefly at two more theories that have been applied recently: the GARCH and Chaos theories.

GARCH theory

GARCH, or Generalised Auto-Regressive Conditional Heteroskedasticity (you can see why people prefer to call it GARCH!), predicts that there are trends in volatility. If a share price has had a large swing on one day, then it will have a large swing on the next. Trends were identified by squaring the returns, which produced an apparent correlation over time. The investment strategy suggested is to purchase options to buy and to sell, thus betting that the stock price would move one way or the other; you would only lose if the stock price remained the same. Other studies, however, have contradicted the GARCH theory: the trends only seem to appear when the market is not very volatile. Thus, GARCH may work, but not all the time.

Chaos theory

Chaos theory was devised to explain the discovery that some apparently complex and random patterns have simple underlying causes, and can be predicted in the short term even though prediction accuracy decreases over time. The spread of disease epidemics and growth patterns of micro-organisms, for example, have been successfully modelled using chaos theory.

Attempts to apply chaos mathematics to the stock market have so far met with only limited success. The idea is to identify periods when the 'Lyapunov time horizon' (the point in the future when a predictable trend disappears) is high, allowing predictions to be made for longer periods than normal. The techniques employ staggeringly large amounts of trading data on computer, and the companies using them are secretive. So far, the consensus is that there may be 'pockets of predictability' that chaos theory can predict, but that the market undergoes frequent changes which disrupt the predictions generated by chaos theory.

Neural networks

Computer programs that are able to spot patterns in the data are increasingly being used in market forecasting. These programs, known as 'neural networks', are a tool in the never-ending trawl of market data in search of relationships and trends. Their popularity has made them affordable. You can now buy neural network software that will run on a personal computer at home.

Neural networks are simply tools, you still need to use judgement to know when and if to exploit the patterns they throw up. For example, they tend to 'overfit'; this means that they often identify patterns that are purely coincidental. It is then up to the operator to weed out such spurious patterns. As computer technology improves, so will the usefulness of neural networks, but the complexity of their operation may keep them in the hands of the biggest traders.

The Efficient Market theory

Throughout most of the history of the stock markets, most people thought that if only you could properly understand the patterns in stock price movements, you could predict how they would move in the future. People like Charles Dow were taken very seriously in their day.

In the late 1950s a young American undergraduate, Eugene Fama, was helping a professor to produce a stock market newsletter. Fama's job was to analyse the historical price data to identify 'buy' and 'sell' signals based on recurring patterns. After a while Fama saw that although you could find repeating patterns, they did not predict future price movements well at all, and later he published an academic paper, 'Random Walks in Stock Market Prices', which suggested that stock price variations were randomly distributed and therefore unpredictable.

Fama was *not* suggesting that most share prices go up and down like yo-yos. Most of the time, the price changes are tiny in the short term. It is these tiny changes, argued Fama, that are random and unpredictable – they take a 'random walk'.

To understand the 'random walk', imagine you're standing in a field, and you flip a coin for each step you take. 'Heads' you turn right, and 'tails' you turn left. After you have taken 25 steps in this way, on average you will be only five steps away from where you started (Figure 7.7). If you were a share price, however, an investor would like to be able to predict the point when you were furthest away from your starting point. Fama said this isn't possible, and proposed that the reason for these price changes were that investors' views are constantly changing in response to the flow of new information about companies and markets.

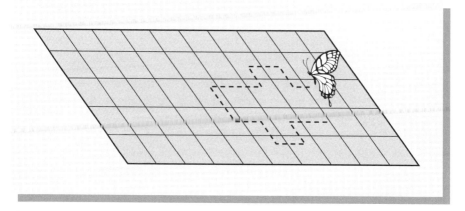

Figure 7.7   A random walk

Whenever there is news affecting a share, fundamental analysts will react immediately, and the share price will adjust very quickly as they trade. The efficient market theory says that it is precisely because fundamental analysts are good at their job that their predictions don't work. The prices of stocks and shares are immediately adjusted as the professionals buy what they think is undervalued and sell what they think is overvalued, leaving the smaller investor as well off by selecting a portfolio by throwing darts at the financial pages as by following the advice of the professionals.

In essence, what the efficient market theory says is that fundamental analysis does not help investors get better returns than if they simply bought shares and held them for a long time. It has been shown, however, that although major stock markets like the ones in the UK and US may be efficient, many of the smaller ones, such as the ones in the Far East, are almost certainly not efficient, and so special expertise may produce unusually good returns in such markets.

In the 1970s, Fama revised his ideas and proposed that market efficiency make take one of the following forms:

▪ **'Weak form'**: past price information is fully reflected in the current price of a share. Patterns in past prices will not help predict future price movements.

▪ **'Semi-strong'** form: the current share price reflects all information contained in past prices and all relevant publicly available information. Fundamental analysis will not help you find a share that is likely to rise more than the market already expects, since the price will already reflect all that is publicly known about the firm.

▪ **'Strong' form**: the current share price reflects all information contained in past prices, all relevant publicly available information, and all other information known by anybody (such as 'insider information'). This means, for instance, that a geologist who has a special understanding of oilfields will not be able to make excess returns consistently because others with a similar understanding will already have bid prices up to a fair level.

The main point to understand is that the efficient market hypothesis does not claim that no one ever earns unusually high, or 'excess' returns. It says that excess returns are randomly distributed.

The efficient market hypothesis has created a lot of interest in index tracking in the US and the UK. This is because funds that are actively managed by professionals do not, overall, produce returns that are even as good as the main market indices (which is pretty good evidence for market efficiency). Many people now argue that:

■ expensive professional analysis and research is wasted;

■ investment professionals do not add value to investments they manage;

■ buying and holding will give better returns to private investors than frequent trading.

Index investing is probably a good approach for private investors, since it is inexpensive and will produce returns that are close to the index you track. If everybody did it, however, it could make the popular indices very volatile, so it is not a strategy that is invulnerable to problems in all circumstances.

Conclusion

Many brokers will tell you that new techniques for predicting the market may work for some time, but as more and more people start to use them they will become less effective. All of the theories that we have looked at in this chapter have probably been effective at one time or another in the history of the stock market. The paradox is that the way that the market is structured seems to protect it against the monopoly of any one method in the long term. If a strategy is working, more and more people start to copy it, and this will reduce or destroy the benefits of the strategy.

8

Probability

Life is full of uncertainty, and so is business. The mathematics of probability helps us to understand uncertainty better, and to reduce risk.

Consider the following four statements:

1 This investment is too good to miss; the potential profits are so great that even if it has only a tiny chance of success, it would be madness to pass it up.

2 I'm not going to visit the UK this year because of all the bombs.

3 I am going to practise celibacy my whole life because of the risk of contracting HIV from having sex. I'm not going to play Russian roulette!

4 I met a woman on the plane whose husband knows my friend Geoff. What an amazing coincidence!

All of these statements display a misunderstanding of probability. Let's examine each one in turn.

Statement 1 ignores the existence of other investment opportunities of equal risk, which, it implies, is high. Should we follow this reasoning and invest a small sum? Perhaps, but it would be safer to invest in a wide range of similar schemes, so that we would spread our risk wider. If the schemes are very risky, though, with a chance of only, say 1 in 10 billion of any one of them succeeding, we would run out of money before we had a reasonable chance of recovering our bets.

Statement 2 refers to a phenomenon that most travellers are familiar with. The news about a country usually makes it sound more dangerous than it really is. This is because news tends to focus on dangerous events. Think about your own neighbourhood: how many terrible things happen there in a year? There is probably more bad news in a year about your town than your neighbourhood, more bad news about your part of the country than your town, more bad news about your country than your part of the country, and more bad international news than home news. We tend to forget that other countries are just like our own: they are made up of separate districts, towns and neighbourhoods too. If a bomb has gone off in, say, London, it doesn't necessarily follow that the danger of terrorist attacks on the village of Catsworth in Cambridgeshire has significantly increased, so it would be silly to abandon a visit to Catsworth (assuming you were not passing through London) on the grounds that there has been a bombing in London.

Statement 3 is a more extreme reaction to the danger of HIV than most doctors recommend. The usual medical advice is always to use a condom when having sex, because it greatly reduces the risk of contracting any sexually transmitted disease. Research suggests that HIV is not highly infectious, with estimates of the risk of transmission during a single act of unprotected heterosexual sex ranging from 1 in 1,000 to 1 in 10,000. The risk of contracting HIV by having unprotected sex once is therefore much lower than playing Russian roulette once (where one bullet is loaded into a six chamber revolver). Using a condom reduces the risk much further. The point of this is not to make light of a tragic disease, nor to comment on current medical knowledge about it, but to show that lifetime celibacy is probably an unreasonably extreme measure to take to avoid HIV.

Statement 4 is perhaps the easiest of the four types of trap to fall into. Suppose you and the lady that you met on the plane are both nationals of a large country with a population of about 200 million adults. Let's say that most adults know about 1,500 people spread around the country. The probability of two individuals being linked by two others is more than 99 in 100, so it is the fact that they discover this in conversation is the surprise, not the existence of the link itself. If you restricted the links to that part of the population that travels by air, the probability of a link of this kind is even higher.

Mathematicians have been studying probability for hundreds of years, prompted at first by their wealthy gambling friends, so many of the problems they have worked on are stated in terms of games of chance, using cards, coins and dice.

Defining probability

Figure 8.1 shows a probability scale. If we give absolute certainty a value of 1, and absolute impossibility a value of 0, you can see that the probability of all uncertain events will fall between 0 and 1. A 3 in 4 chance of an event occurring is the same as a 0.75 chance and is readily converted into a percentage – in this case, 75%.

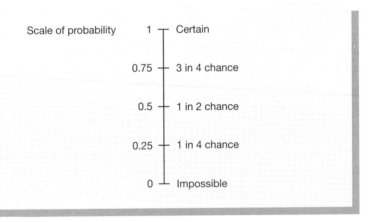

Figure 8.1   Scale of probability

Example

You flip a coin. What is the chance that it will land showing heads? There are only two possibilities, heads or tails, so the chance of flipping heads is 1 in 2, or 50%, assuming that the coin is 'fair', in other words, that the coin is not weighted or shaped to favour a particular side. If you have to predict the outcome before you flip the coin, you will either be right or wrong, but if you flip the coin many times, you will be able to guess how many times heads will turn up with some accuracy. In fact, the more times that you flip the coin, the smaller the percentage of error in your over-all prediction will get. If you flip the coin 10,000 times, and guess that you will get heads 5,000 times, you will probably be out by a very small percentage.

The 'law of large numbers' states that if you flipped the coin a very large number of times, you would get heads almost exactly 50% of the time overall. The trouble is that you can't flip the coin an infinite number of times, so you will probably always be a little bit out in your predictions. In business, however, being slightly out on a prediction is much better than not being able to predict at all, so probability is extremely useful.

Measuring probability

If all the possible results can be worked out, you can express the probability of a particular result quite easily. Suppose you want to know the probability of getting exactly one head when you flip a fair coin twice. The possible results are:

HH or TT or TH or HT

There are four possible outcomes, all equally likely. Two of them, HT and TH, give you one head, so the probability is 2 in 4, or 50%.

Suppose you want to know the probability of getting exactly two tails when you flip a coin three times. The possible results are:

HHH HTH HHT THH TTH THT HTT TTT

There are eight possible outcomes, of which three give you two tails. Thus, the probability is 3 in 8, or 37.5%. Another way of calculating the probability is to say that since there are eight possible outcomes, all equally likely, the probability for any one of them occurring is 1 in 8. Since three of the outcomes give you two tails, the probability is 1/8 + 1/8 + 1/8 = 3/8 = 37.5%.

Working out the probability of exactly two tails *not* occurring is easy. Just subtract the previous result from 1 or if you are using percentages, subtract from 100:

$$1 - 3/8 = 5/8$$

$$100 - 37.5 = 62.5\%$$

If you are working out the probability that an event will not occur, it is often easier to work out the probability of it occurring, and then obtain the result by subtraction as we have just done.

If you have to work out the probability when there are many possible outcomes, writing them all out and counting them can be very laborious, so it is better to use a formula. To work out the probability, called P, of a particular event, called A, the formula is:

$$P(A) = n(A) \div n$$

n(A) represents the number of outcomes when A occurs, and n represents the total number of outcomes.

Example

> You have a pack of playing cards and you want to know the chances of drawing
> any court card in spades. There are 52 cards in a pack, and 3 court cards in spades
> (Jack, Queen and King), so using the formula you can work out that:
>
> P(any court card in spades) = 3 ÷ 52 = 5.77%

So far, so good, but what if you can't easily spot the number of possible outcomes?

Ways of counting

There are three main ways of counting possible outcomes, *multiplication*, *permutations* and *combinations*.

Multiplication

Suppose you have three dice, coloured red, blue and green respectively. How many possible outcomes are there? You know the possible outcomes for any one of the dice, which is six, so to get the total, you multiply outcomes for each die together:

$$6 \times 6 \times 6 = 216$$

There are 216 possible outcomes.

If you had 25 dice, it would be easier to work out the outcomes as 6^{25} using a calculator:

$$6^{25} = 28{,}430{,}288{,}029{,}929{,}701{,}376$$

Conditional probability

The multiplication rule only works when the events are independent of one another. Suppose you throw the red die and the blue die together and you want to know the probability of the red die showing 3 (A), and the blue die showing any even number (B); these events are tied together, or 'conditional', and can be written as:

$$P(A \cap B) = P(B, \text{ given A occurs}) \times P(A)$$

The symbol $\cap$ joins A and B, and means that we want to know the probability of both A and B occurring. We calculate the answer as:

$$P(A) = 1/6$$
$$P(B \text{ given that A occurs}) = 3/6 = 1/2$$
$$P(B \text{ given that A occurs}) \times P(A) = 1/6 \times 1/2 = 1/12$$
$$P(A \cap B) = 1/12$$

Example

You run a computer software company, and you have just developed a new program for business PC users. You estimate that the probability of showing a profit in the first year is 80%, but only if your major competitor does not come out with a similar product. If the competitor does introduce a similar product, you think that the probability that you will make a profit will fall to 40%. You also estimate that the chance that the competitor will indeed introduce a rival program is 1 in 2, or 50%.

Suppose that:

Event A is the competitor introducing the rival program, and Event B is your program showing a profit in the first year if A occurs. You want to know the probability of A and B occurring together.

$$P(A) = 50\%, \text{ or } 0.5$$
$$P(B \text{ given that A occurs}) = 40\%, \text{ or } 0.4$$
$$P(B \text{ given that A doesn't occur}) = 0.8$$

Using the formula, we see that:

$$P(A \cap B) = 0.5 \times 0.4 = 0.2$$

There is a 20% probability of showing a profit in the first year and your competitor introducing a rival product.

Permutations

Multiplication works when there are several events, each of which have a known number of outcomes which are independent of the others, but often we find situations when this is not the case. Suppose you want to know how many possible six-digit telephone numbers there are in which no digit is repeated. These rearrangements are called 'permutations'.

The first digit has 10 possible numbers:

$$0, 1, 2, 3, 4, 5, 6, 7, 8, 9$$

and the second digit must have one less possible numbers than the first, (i.e. 9), the third digit has eight possible numbers and so on; to work them out, you use factorials (see page 192) and the formula:

$$^nP_r = n! \div (n - r)!$$

where n is the number of objects (in this case the 10 possible numbers 0 to 9), and r is the number of objects to be arranged from n, (in this case the six digits of the phone number).

$$^{10}P_6 = 10! \div (10 - 6)!$$
$$= 3{,}628{,}800 \div 4!$$
$$= 3{,}628{,}800 \div 24$$
$$= 151{,}200$$

There are 151,200 ways of arranging a six-digit telephone number without repeating any digit.

Combinations of probabilities

If you want to select r number of objects from a set of n objects and the order doesn't matter, you are 'combining' r objects. The formula for this is:

$$^nC_r = n! \div r!(n - r)!$$

Notice that the difference between this and the previous formula is that in this case you multiply the last term $(n - r)!$ by $r!$.

Example

You are playing poker, and are dealt a hand of five cards. How many possible hands (combinations of five cards) could you be dealt? And what are the chances of getting four aces? These are two separate questions, the first of which can be solved with the formula for combinations. Work out how many possible hands you could be dealt:

n is the number of cards in a pack, 52; and
r is the number of cards in a hand, 5:
number of hands $^{52}C_5 = 52! \div 5!(52 - 5)!$
$$= 52! \div (5! \times 47!)$$
$$= 52! \div (120 \times 47!)$$
$$= 2{,}598{,}960$$

There are 2,598,960 possible hands of five cards from a 52-card pack that has no jokers.

To work out your chance of being dealt four aces in your five-card hand, we use the first probability formula in the section, $P(A) = n(A) \div n$.

The probability (P) of getting four aces (A) equals the number of ways of dealing a hand of four aces and one other card n(A), divided by the total number of possible hands, n. We have just worked out n; to work out n(A), think of it like this:

Ace Ace Ace Ace plus one other card

There are 48 other cards in the pack, so there are 48 possible hands with four aces.

$$n(A) = 48.$$
Using $P(A) = n(A) \div n$,
$$P(A) = 48 \div 2{,}598{,}960 = 0.0000185, \text{ or } 0.00185\%$$

There is a 0.00185% chance of being dealt four aces.

Combinations or permutations?

Sometimes it is a bit hard to spot whether you should be using the combination formula or the permutation formula. You may find it helps to think of a horse race.

Suppose there are four horses in a race and you want to bet that certain horses will get in the top three. Instead of names, the horses have numbers, 1, 2, 3 and 4. These are all the possible combinations of horses in the top three:

$$123 \quad 124 \quad 234 \quad 134$$

These are *combinations* because the order is not specified.

Now suppose you want to bet both that horses 1, 2 and 3 are going to be the top three, and to bet on the order in which they will come in.

The possible ways they could come in are:

$$123 \quad 132 \quad 213 \quad 231 \quad 312 \quad 321$$

These are *permutations* because the order is important.

Notice that while there are only four possible combinations of any three of the four horses, there are six permutations of each of the four combinations, giving:

$$6 \times 4 = 24 \text{ possible permutations in all.}$$

Conditional probability

Conditional probability refers to cases when you want to know the probability of an event given that another event has occurred.

Example

Suppose that your company makes two kinds of china plates, standard and deluxe. The VAT inspector has made a surprise visit, and is checking through the sales records for June. There are 433 invoices issued in June, of which 300 are to retailers and 133 are to wholesalers. Of the 300 invoices to retailers, 82 are for standard plates, and of the 133 invoices to wholesalers, 30 are for standard plates. The inspector picks a wholesale invoice (W) at random. What are the chances that it is for deluxe plates (D)?

To write this question in mathematical form, we use a vertical line | to mean 'given that'. The probability of D occuring given that W has occurred is written as P(D | W).

There are 133 wholesale invoices (W) or possible events, of which 133 − 30 = 103 are for deluxe plates (D). You work out the probability like this:

$$P(D \mid W) = 103 \div 133 = 0.77$$

There is a 0.77, or 77%, chance that the VAT inspector will pick an invoice for deluxe plates. The general formula for conditional probability is P(D | W) = P(A ∩ B) ÷ P(B). Remember that the ∩ sign means 'joined with'.

Dependent events

In the previous example of the VAT inspector choosing an invoice, the two events, picking one for deluxe plates, and picking one to a wholesaler are said to be 'dependent', because we wanted to know the chances that the inspector would pick an invoice for deluxe plates given that a wholesale invoice had been chosen. If we just wanted to know the chances of the inspector picking any wholesale invoice and then any deluxe plate invoice, the two events would not be dependent on one another.

Independent events

If you have two events occurring simultaneously, they may be independent of each other. For example, if you flip two coins, the chances of getting tails on each coin are independent, since one coin does not affect the other, so the probability can be obtained by multiplication:

$$1/2 \times 1/2 = 1/4.$$

Another way of defining independence is to say that A is independent of B if:

$$P(A \mid B) = P(A)$$
$$\text{and}$$
$$P(B \mid A) = P(B)$$

Example

Suppose that a group of managers claims that they have been passed over for promotion because they are members of a particular ethnic minority group (let's call it 'Ruritanians') and makes a formal complaint of unlawful discrimination. The managers accept that their employer has increased the number of managers who are also members of their ethnic group, but they say that they seem to stay in junior jobs while others get promoted. As evidence, they point out that during the past five years only 12 of 79 promotions went to Ruritanians.

The HR department replies that there are far fewer Ruritanian managers than others, and that managers aren't usually promoted in the first year, which accounts for the lack of promotion of the newer Ruritanian managers. The department produces Table 8.1 which classifies managers employed for over a year according to ethnic grouping, and says that managers have been promoted without regard to ethnicity. Is the HR department correct?

Table 8.1 Managers employed for more than a year by ethnic grouping

Manager	*Promoted*	*Not promoted*	*Total*
Ruritanian	12	47	59
Non-Ruritanian	69	276	345
Total	81	323	404

The probability of a non Ruritanian manager being promoted is 69 ÷ 345 = 0.2

The probability of a Ruritanian manager being promoted is 12 ÷ 47 = 0.255

The probability overall of all managers being promoted is 81 ÷ 404 = 0.2

If anything, the Ruritanian managers have had a slightly better chance of being promoted than the non-Ruritanian managers.

Mutually exclusive events

If you flip a coin three times, the probability of getting three tails is 1 in 8, and the probability of getting two tails is 1 in 4, but they can't both happen, so they are called mutually exclusive events.

Non-exclusive events

If you draw a black jack from a pack of cards, the probability is 1/52 + 1/52 = 1/25 because there are two black jacks. If you draw any spade from the pack, the probability is 13 ÷ 52 because there are 13 spades.

What is the probability of drawing a black jack or any spade card? The answer is NOT 1/25 + 13/52 = 15/52 = 0.288, because the 13 spades include the jack of spades, so you would be counting it twice.

The answer can be worked out by calculating the probability of drawing a jack of spades, 1/52, and subtracting it from 1/25 + 13/52:

$$(1/25 + 13/52) - 1/52 = 14/52 = 0.269$$

Probability trees

If you want to work out the probability of several events occurring, it often helps to draw a tree of all the possible events. Figure 8.2 shows a probability tree for all the possible events when you flip a coin twice.

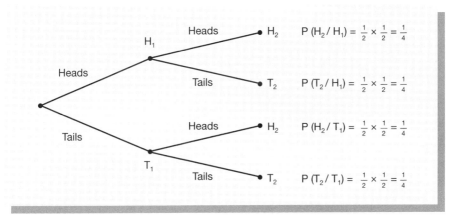

Figure 8.2   Probability tree for the possible results of flipping a coin twice

There are four possible events:

Heads on the first flip (H1).
Tails on the first flip (T1).
Heads on the second flip (H2).
Tails on the second flip (T2).

There are four possible outcomes:

Heads, heads (H2 | H1).
Heads, tails (T2 | H1).
Tails, heads (H2 | TI).
Tails, tails (T2 | T1).

You would not need to draw a probability tree to work out the answers for this situation, but they can be very useful in more complicated problems.

Example

You are the manager of a department store, and you are examining the buying patterns of customers in the shoe section. You know that the probability of a customer buying a pair of shoes (S) after entering the section is 0.4 = P(S). If a customer buys a pair of shoes, there is a 0.5 chance that shoe cream (C) will also be purchased, P(C | S) = 0.5. If the customer does not buy a pair of shoes, there is a 0.1 chance that shoe cream will be purchased, P(C | $\bar{S}$) = 0.1.

Find the probability of the following:

Purchase of a pair of shoes P(S).

Purchase of a pair of shoes and shoe cream.

Purchase of either a pair of shoes or shoe cream.

Purchase of shoe cream.

We know that P(S) = 0.4, P(C | S) = 0.5 and P(C | $\bar{S}$) = 0.1 where $\bar{S}$ means the customer doesn't buy shoes.

Starting with the unconditional event that a customer buys a pair of shoes, we can now draw the probability tree in Figure 8.3.

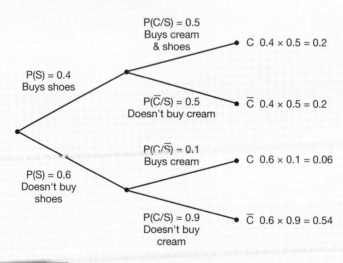

Figure 8.3   **A probability tree for shoes and shoe-cream customer**

In Figure 8.3, we calculated $P(\bar{C} \mid S)$ by subtracting $P(C \mid S) = 0.5$ from 1, and we calculated $P(\bar{C} \mid \bar{S})$ by subtracting $P(C \mid \bar{S}) = 0.1$ from 1.

Now we can work out that:

The probability of the customer buying shoes and cream is 0.4 x 0.5 = 0.2.

The probability of the customer buying cream is 0.2 + 0.06 = 0.26.

The probability of the customer buying shoes or cream is 0.2 + 0.2 + 0.06 = 0.46.

The probability of the customer buying cream only is 0.06.

Estimating probability

It is often not possible to know as much about a problem of chance as we do when we flip a coin, so we have to guess. If you are supplying computer chips, and you tested a batch of 1,000 and found that 60 were faulty, you could guess that the probability of any individual getting a faulty chip from you is 60 in 1000, or 6%. This is sampling, which we looked at in Chapter 1.

Common mistakes in calculating probability

Like most skills, working out probability gets easier the more you practise. Here are some common mistakes that people make in their calculations:

▪ If there are n possible events, each event has a probability of $1 \div n$ only when the events are equally likely.

If you roll two dice, there are 11 possible results:

1 + 1 = 2, 1 + 2 = 3, 1 + 3 = 4, 1 + 4 = 5, 1 + 5 = 6, 1 + 6 = 7
2 + 1 = 3, 2 + 2 = 4, 2 + 3 = 5, 2 + 4 = 6, 2 + 5 = 7, 2 + 6 = 8
3 + 1 = 4, 3 + 2 = 5, 3 + 3 = 6, 3 + 4 = 7, 3 + 5 = 8, 3 + 6 = 9
4 + 1 = 5, 4 + 2 = 6, 4 + 3 = 7, 4 + 4 = 8, 4 + 5 = 9, 4 + 6 = 10
5 + 1 = 6, 5 + 2 = 7, 5 + 3 = 8, 5 + 4 = 9, 5 + 5 = 10, 5 + 6 = 11
6 + 1 = 7, 6 + 2 = 8, 6 + 3 = 9, 6 + 4 = 10, 6 + 5 = 11, 6 + 6 = 12

From this you can see that, for example, a result of 12 is less likely than a result of 3, and both are less likely than a result of 7, so neither of them have a probability of 1 in 11.

▪ You can only add probabilities if the events are exclusive of one another. Generally, $P(A \text{ or } B) \leq P(A) + P(B)$.

▪ You can only multiply probabilities when the events are independent of one another.

▪ Dependence does not imply causation.

For example, the probability of a person playing rugby (R), given that the person is called Tom (T) is not the same as the probability that a person plays rugby.

$P(R \mid T)$ does not equal $P(R)$, since British men are more likely to play rugby than people in general, and British men are more likely to be called Tom than people in general. However, it would be foolish to deduce that people play rugby because they are called Tom.

Similarly, $P(T \mid R)$ does not equal $P(T)$. The probability of a person being called Tom given that they play rugby is not the same as the probability of a person being called Tom, and it is even more foolish to say that they are called Tom *because* they play rugby. As the first example shows, the time is not the important thing; the probability is just concerned with a world full of people, some called Tom and some playing rugby.

Conclusion

Probability theory underlies much of the statistical methods used in the modern world, from insurance to medical treatment, but we rarely find questions of probability in a pure form, except in games of chance. More often, we don't really know enough about a situation to be able to make a really precise calculation of the probabilities. For example, in the example on page 180, the manager estimated the probability of a competitor coming out with a rival product. Unless the manager has a spy in the competitor's boardroom, this estimate may be little more than supposition. Similarly, if you are applying for a job and the ratio of applicants to hirings is 10:1, does this really mean that you have a 1 in 10 chance of getting the job? What if you are completely unqualified for the job – wouldn't this reduce the probability, and if so, by how much, exactly?

Real-life situations are generally too complex for us to calculate the probabilities precisely. However, modelling how the situation might work, given certain assumptions, helps us to think about the probabilities more clearly. Often, making estimates of probabilities highlights the areas of the problem that we don't know enough about, and indicates what we need to research in order to obtain a better estimate of the probabilities. So don't just accept the first estimate you make of the probabilities in a given situation: the more you can find out, the better your estimates will become.

Appendix
Basic concepts and notation

In the main text of the book, some familiarity with basic maths is assumed. In this appendix we will look at notation (signs and symbols that are used to represent processes), and also at some basic mathematical concepts, so if you ran across something that seemed completely new, or you can't quite remember how it works, you should find the explanation here. In any case, unless you work with maths regularly, or have recently passed a maths exam, it should be worthwhile reading through to jog your memory.

Mathematical notation: a refresher

Before we start on notation, here are a few tips for solving problems that often occur when you are doing basic sums.

Addition: solving a book-keeping problem

You've laboriously added all the figures in a ledger, and the two columns don't balance. You may have just made a mistake in your addition, or you could have made errors of omission or have an entry with the decimal point in the wrong place. Often a figure is entered with one or more fewer decimal places on one side than on the other. Check the difference between the two sums of the columns. Is it divisible by 9 or 99? If it is, the chances are that a figure has been transposed.

Example

The difference between your debit and credit columns is 50,597.91, and you can't find out why.

Step 1. Divide the difference by 99.

50,597.91 ÷ 99 = 511.09.

Step 2. Check the ledger for a figure that has been recorded as 51,109 on one side and 511.09 on the other. If you find it, you've solved the problem.

Omission is simply leaving out a number in one column that has been recorded in the other. In the example above, you would have first checked for omission by seeing if the difference between the two columns, 50,597.91, turned up in one of the columns and not the other.

Multiplication

There are three ways to write multiplication:

$$5 \times 6 = 30$$
$$5 * 6 = 30$$
$$5 . 5 = 30.$$

The last way can be confused with a decimal point. The only way to tell is by the context, so be careful – it is commonly used in many countries.

The result of multiplication is called the product. Remember that $5 \times 6 \times 2$ is just the same as $(5 \times 6) \times 2$. In algebra, a letter multiplied by a number is usually written without a multiplication sign; for example 6 times A, where A = income, is written 6, not $6 \times A$.

Negative numbers

Negative numbers are numbers less than 0. When two negative numbers are multiplied, the result is positive: $-2 \times -2 = 4$. This means that the square of a negative number is always positive. Dividing a positive number by a negative number gives a negative result: $4 \div -2 = -2$.

Decimals and fractions

Fractions

20 out of 80 employees in a company are female. $20/80 = 2/8 = 1/4$; these are fractions, or 'vulgar fractions'. Always check if the top and bottom of a fraction can be made smaller by division. You could say that two-eighths of the staff are female, but it would be better to say that a quarter are female. If you wanted to express 1/4 as a decimal figure, all you have to remember is that the first place to the right of the decimal point is tenths, the second is hundredths, and so on. To convert 1/4 to decimals, divide the top number, called the numerator, by the bottom number, called the denominator:

$$1.00 \div 4 = 0.25$$

Decimals

'Decimal places' are the number of places to the right of the decimal point of your number; zeros on the end don't count, unless they are there for a special reason not covered here. 2.2 has one decimal place, 2.22 has two decimal places, and so on. The number 2.220 should usually be written 2.22, since the 0 on the end doesn't make any difference to its value. Most currencies have two decimal places, so if, for instance, 2.20 referred to pounds and pence, you would write it as 2.20, not 2.2.

Circles

If you want to draw accurate pie charts (see page 60), remember that there are 360 degrees in a circle, and to measure them you need a protractor, which is a kind of ruler for circles and angles. If you have a computer with desktop publishing software, you should be able to measure circles without one.

In Figure A.1 you can see the names of the basic parts of a circle. The radius is the line between the centre and any point on the circumference, the circumference is the line that forms the circle, and the diameter is a line cutting the circle into equal halves (and is therefore twice the length of the radius).

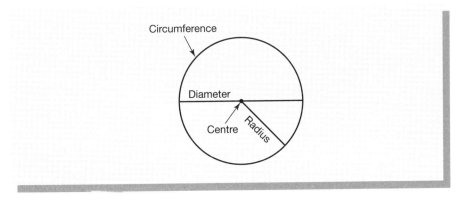

Figure A.1   Parts of a circle

Pi (π)

π is the Greek letter 'p' and is pronounced 'pi' (like 'pie'). You may come across it being used to mean two completely different things.

When dealing with circles, π is the length of the circumference of any circle divided by the diameter of that circle, and is always the same number, which is equal to 3.142 to 3 decimal places. π is an 'irrational number' which goes on for ever without repeating a pattern; it can't be expressed exactly as a fraction or a decimal. Another approximation of π is 22/7; this number also goes on for ever, but it is not exactly the same number as it, and it is not irrational, because it repeats the sequence of numbers 142857:

$$22 \div 7 = 3.142857142857142857142857$$

Some US states actually passed laws to define π as 22/7 or, in one case, 3!

In statistics, π is sometimes used to mean the proportion of a population. These two meanings for it are so different that you won't be confused about which one is intended.

Factorials

The factorial of a number is the product of all the whole numbers from 1 up to and including the number in question, and is denoted by the symbol !, e.g. factorial 4 is written as 4!

$$4! = 4 \times 3 \times 2 \times 1 = 24.$$

Strangely, 0! is given the value of 1. This makes some useful formulae work in extra cases, and has no greater significance than this.

Equalities, inequalities, greater than and less than

The 'equals' sign is written as =.

'Almost equals' is written as ≈. For instance, 6.01≈ 6.

'Greater than' is written as >, and 'greater than or equal to' is written as ≥.

'Less than' is <, and 'less than or equal to' is ≤.

Example

> 5 million > 4 million.
> 4 million < 5 million.
> 5 > 4, and 4 < 5.

Intervals

An interval is the set of numbers between any two given numbers. The set may or may not include both or either of the two end points. Figure A.2 shows three kinds of interval.

The interval between 2 and 7, including both 2 and 7, is called a closed interval and is written as [2, 7] or $2 \leq \chi \leq 7$.

The interval which includes all the numbers between 2 and 7 except for 2 and 7, is called an open interval and is written [2, 7], $2 < \times < 7$, or sometimes (2, 7).

The interval which includes all the numbers between 2 and 7 and includes *either* 2 or 7 is called a half-open interval. If it includes 2 and excludes 7, it is written [2, 7[, or $2 \leq \chi < 7$, or [2, 7). Remember that intervals include all the possible numbers, including those that are not whole numbers, between the numbers too.

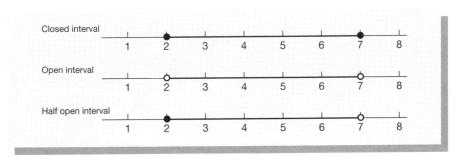

Figure A.2   Intervals

Brackets

Brackets are used in calculations to show which part of the calculation should be done first. If no brackets are used, it is conventional to multiply and divide before adding and subtracting.

Example

You are asked to calculate $5 + 4 \times 3 \div 2 - 5$.

Which of the following is the correct answer?

$$(9 \times 1.5) - 5 = 8.5$$
$$5 + (12 \div -3) = 1$$
$$5 + (4 \times 1.5) - 5 = 6$$
$$(5 + 4) \times (3 \div -3) = -9$$

You could try using the convention, but the chances are that whoever wrote the sum down without bothering to use brackets probably wasn't thinking about conventions either. To find the solution, you would have to know more about how the person got to the calculation in the first place.

If it had been written as $5 + \{(4 \times 3) \div (2 - 5)\}$, life would be easier, since you would then work out the answers to the items within the brackets first:

$$5 + \{(4 \times 3) \div (2 - 5)\} = 5 + (12 \div -3) = 5 + (-4) = 1$$

Round brackets are usually used in equations such as the one above, and for the coordinates on graphs; (1, 3) means 1 on the horizontal (x) axis, and 3 on the vertical (y) axis. Sometimes, when there are many nested sets of brackets, other brackets are used so that it is easier to see which left bracket goes with which right bracket:

Squiggly brackets are often used for sets of numbers, such as {5,7,10}.

Square brackets are used to show intervals; [2,5] means that $2 \leq \chi \leq 5$.

Square brackets used like this:]2,5[mean $2 < \chi < 5$.

Square brackets used like this:]2,5] mean $2 < \chi \leq 5$.

Percentages

A percentage is another way of writing a fraction with a denominator of 100. 8% is the same as $8 \div 100$. 8.5% is the same as (8.5 ± 100). Any fraction can be written as a percentage, but it is surprising how many people calculate them wrongly.

Example

You are offered £91 commission on a product that sells for £832. What percentage commission are you getting?

Step 1. Your commission is the fraction 91/832 of the price. The percentage can be expressed as:

$$91/832 \times 100 = 9100/832$$

Step 2. Divide 9,100 by 832 = 10.93. You are getting 10.93% commission.

Perhaps the reason why people make mistakes when calculating percentages is that they think that since they are taking a percentage of the larger figure, they should multiply the larger figure (in our example 832) by 100, or else that the larger figure should be divided by the smaller figure. If you sometimes make mistakes like this, just remember to think of the calculation as a fraction, and multiply the top number by 100.

Example

Suppose you are offered a product at 17.5% off its quoted price of £1,548. How much discount are you getting?

Step 1. Turn this into an equation, where x is the discount in pounds:

$$(x \div 1,548) \times 100 = 17.5.$$

Step 2. 100x = 17.5 × 1,548 = 27,090.

Step 3. x = 27,090 ÷ 100 = 270.90.

You are getting a discount of £270.90.

Errors with percentages

As well as the commonly made errors in calculating percentages, there are people in this world who deliberately use them incorrectly, usually in order to confuse a customer about price. To use a petty example, suppose the exchange rate for Doubloons to Escudos changes from D 1 : E 4 to D 1 : E 8.

A sign outside a bureau de change tells you that the escudo has fallen by 100%. Is this true? No; a fall of 100% means a fall to 0. The D has risen by 100% in relation to the E, since the increase is 4 E, which expressed as a percentage of the original 4 is 100%, but the E has fallen by only 50%, which you can work out by expressing the ratios in the form of what 1 Escudo is worth:

The original rate was E 1 : D ¼.

It dropped to E 1 : D 1/8, so the Escudo has dropped by 50% in its buying power of Doubloons.

Another example of confusion is 'price = 120 including 20% commission'. This usually means 'original price = 100 + 20% commission = 120', but it could mean 'commission = 20% × 120 = 24', so the original price is 120 − 24 = 96. This kind of confusion often arises in prices subject to VAT: is the price quoted including VAT or excluding VAT?

Calculating VAT

Value Added Tax, or VAT, is a tax on the sale of certain goods. Governments sometimes change the rate of VAT; the standard rate used to be 17.5% in the UK, but is currently 20%. Let's use the old rate of 17.5% to make the sums a little harder.

If a price is quoted as £470 excluding VAT, calculate the total including VAT using the formula $x = (n \times 17.5) \div 100$, where x is the VAT amount and n is the price excluding VAT.

$$x = (470 \times 17.5) \div 100$$
$$= 82.25$$

The VAT on £470 is £82.25, so the price including VAT is £470 + £82.25 = £552.25.

Powers and roots

Multiplying a number by itself several times is called raising it to a power:

$$2 \times 2 \times 2 = 8 \text{ is the same as } 2^3$$

You have multiplied 2 by itself 3 times, or raised 2 to the power of 3. Raising a number to the power of 3 is called cubing, and raising a number to the power of 2 is called squaring. It is easier to write large numbers by indicating the power than to write them out completely:

For example, 10,000,000,000 is the same as 10^{10}.

▥ If the power, or exponent, is a minus number, it means that the whole figure is divided into 1: 2^{-2} is the same as $2^{1/2}$, which is ¼.

▥ It is useful to express both very large and very small numbers in terms of powers because it makes them more convenient to write. Thus 0.000034 can be written as 34×10^{-6}, and 34,500,000,000 can be written as 34×10^8. This is called 'scientific notation'.

▥ If the exponent is 1/x, it means 'take the root'. $4^{1/2}$ means 'take the square root of 4', which is 2.

▥ If you want to multiply the same number to different powers by itself, you simply add the powers. For example, $2^9 \times 2^3 = 2^{9+3} = 2^{12}$.

Roots are the opposite of powers. The convention is to write square roots as x where x is any number, and to write the root number in front of the sign for any other root; thus, $\sqrt{4} = 2$ and $3\sqrt{8} = 2$. Roots are sometimes called 'fractional powers'.

Using a calculator

Most calculators will work out powers and roots for you. In the old days you had to use tables. The button for working out powers is usually marked x^y or y^x and the button for working out roots are usually marked $y\sqrt{x}$ or $x\sqrt{y}$.

 Some calculators display very large and small numbers using scientific notation. For example, if your calculator displays 2.993 – 04, it means $2.993 \times 10^{-4} = 0.0002993$. With most calculators, if you then pressed + 1, you would get 1.0002993, which is a quick way of remembering where the decimal place should go.

Σ (sigma)

Σ is the Greek capital letter 'S'. It is used in maths to mean the sum of a set of numbers added together. For example, if you could write 'the sum of all business travel expenses incurred' as 'Σ business travel'.

Awkwardly, Σ is also sometimes used to represent the mean and the standard deviation; you should be able to tell which one is meant by the context.

Large numbers

Large numbers are much used in business, but few of us have much of an intuitive notion of what they mean, because the vast scale is unfamiliar to us in daily life. Having an idea of scale is behind many of the great scientific discoveries. For example, a key part of Darwin's argument for evolution in *The Origin of Species* was his idea that creatures evolve over vast periods of time. If you only had a vague idea, as many did at the time, that the world began a few thousand years ago, you would have trouble with the idea of evolution.

The speed of light is 300,000 kilometres per second; a cube with sides a tenth of the diameter of a proton (a subatomic particle) would have sides of 10^{-13} centimetres; the universe is about 15 billion years old. It can be calculated that less than 10^{42} units of the time it takes for light to travel along such a cube have occurred since the beginning of time. A computer cannot calculate faster than this unit of time, so it would take it longer than the history of time for it to calculate 10^{42} steps.

What has all this got to do with business? Apart from the fact that more mundane problems also involve such vast numbers, its general relevance is that if you believe that being able to think for yourself is advantageous in business, then it is worthwhile developing a grasp of how to work with large numbers.

Billions

The two different definitions of a billion sometimes cause confusion; in the UK, a billion used to mean a million million, or 1,000,000,000,000, while in the US, a billion means a thousand million, or 1,000,000,000. The American definition of a billion has largely superseded the British one.

Googol

You should never need to use a googol – it's the name for 10^{100}. The search engine Google is named after this number.

Rounding off

Suppose your department's budget for next year is £120,742.13. Would you tell colleagues that 'the budget figure is one hundred and twenty thousand, seven hundred and forty-two pounds and thirteen pence'? You would if they wanted an exact figure, but if they didn't, you might simply say that lie figure was 'roughly 120,000'; this is called rounding off. In this case, you have rounded off to the nearest 10,000; if you had said '121,000', you would have rounded off to the nearest 1,000, since 120,743.13 is nearer to 121,000 than it is to 120,000. It is a convention that if the digit to the right of the digit you are rounding off to is 5 or above, you round up, and if it is between 0 and 4, you round down. For example, 2.3529 could be rounded off to:

2.353 (three decimal places); or

2.35 (two decimal places); or

2.4 (one decimal place); or even to

2 (the nearest whole number).

The main points to remember are:

- Stick to your own rule. If you're rounding to two decimal places, be consistent. If you make calculations using rounded figures, round the answers to the same number of decimal places. For example, when you multiply the rounded numbers 3.45 and 7.21 you get $3.45 \times 7.21 = 24.8745$. This should be rounded off to 24.87, or else errors will start to creep in as you make further calculations.

- There is money to be made in rounding wherever people seek profit from tiny margins; if you make 0.02 of a penny in the pound in a currency exchange, and you change £200 million, you make 4 million pennies, or £40,000. These things start to matter if you do them frequently.

Significant figures

This is a related idea to rounding off. 94,320 can be written as 94,300 correct to three significant figures, as 94,000 correct to two significant figures, and so on. The significant figures are counted from the first digit in the number that is not 0; thus, 0.0865 is written as 0.09 correct to one significant figure and as 0.087 correct to two significant figures. Remember, when rounding off or using significant figures, you should always try to establish, for yourself and others, what has been done with the numbers so that interpretations and calculations can be rechecked for accuracy.

Logarithms (logs)

Logarithms were invented in the nineteenth century, before people had calculators, to make it easier to do multiplication and division. If you write 1,000 as 10^3, 3 is the log of 1,000 to base 10. If you write 64 as 2^6, 6 is the log of 64 to base 2. If you can write a number as x^y, then y is the log of the number to base x. There are published log tables which you can use to look up the log of a number. Slide rules use logs too.

Example

To use logs to calculate 311 × 574, first convert the numbers to logs:

$$311 = 10^{2.4928} \text{ and } 574 = 10^{2.7589}$$

Therefore:

$$311 \times 574 = 10^{2.4928} \times 10^{2.7589}$$
$$= 10^{2.4928+2.7589}$$
$$= 10^{5.2517}$$

Looking up $10^{5.2517}$ in the antilog tables, we get the answer 178,500, so 311 × 574 = 178,500. When you know the log of a number, as we now do for 178,500, the figure you get from the log tables is called the 'antilogarithm' or 'antilog'. The antilog of $10^{5.2517}$ is 178,500.

We saw that log 574 = $10^{2.7589}$. You can also say that log 574 = 2.7589. The part of the log before (to the left of) the decimal point, in this case 2, is called the 'characteristic' of the logarithm, and the part after the decimal point, in this case .7589, is called the 'mantissa'.

Using a calculator for logs

Calculators often have a button for calculating logs to base 10, which is usually marked LOG.

Equations

As we have already seen, letters are often used to represent numbers which we haven't yet worked out (called 'unknowns'). You could say 2 + x = 4 before you calculated that x = 2. Letters are very useful in equations. Any relationship between numbers that has an equals sign in it is an equation. 2 + 2 = 4 is an equation, and so is x = 2ab ÷ 72.

Equation arithmetic

If you do anything to the numbers on one side of an equation, such as adding or subtracting a number, you must do the same thing to the other side of the equals sign as well, otherwise the two sides will no longer be equal. In the equation $x = y + 77$, you can find what y equals by subtracting 77 from both sides:

$$x = y + 77$$
$$x - 77 = (y + 77) - 77$$
$$x - 77 = y$$

The same principle applies for dividing and multiplying. In the equation $77y = x$, you can find what y equals by dividing both sides by 77:

$$77 \times y = x$$
$$(77 \times y) \div 77 = x \div 77$$
$$Y = x \div 77$$

Sometimes you have lots of brackets in an equation. You should simplify these as much as possible. In the equation $(2y + 56) - (73 + 2)(5 + 2) = x \div [(8 - 3) + 12]$, simplify it as follows:

$$(2y + 56) - (73 + 2)(5 + 2) = x \div [(8 - 3) + 12]$$
$$(2y + 56) - (73 \times 7) = x \div (5 + 12)$$
$$(2y + 56) - 525 = x \div 17$$
$$2y - 469 = x \div 17$$
$$2y = (x \div 17) + 469$$
$$y = (x \div 34) + 234.5$$

You could simplify it further by finding what x equals:

$$x = (y - 234.5) \div 34$$
$$x = 34y - 7973$$

Graphs

A graph is a way of showing information as a picture so that it is easier to understand. The graph that you are probably most familiar with has a vertical scale and a horizontal scale, as in Figure A.3. It was invented by the philosopher René Descartes, famous for the proposition, 'I think, therefore I am', so it is called 'Cartesian' after him.

The horizontal scale is called the x axis and the vertical scale is called the y axis. The points A and B which are marked on the graph have exact positions and can be described by coordinates. The coordinates of A are (1,1) and the coordinates of 13 are (4,5). When you write coordinates, you always put the coordinate of the x axis first and the y axis second.

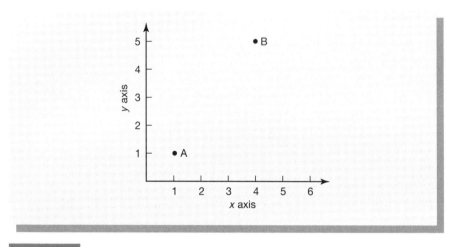

Figure A.3   The Cartesian x + y graph

As we saw in Chapter 3, the scales of the axes don't have to be the same as each other. For example, you could have the x axis marked in thousands and the y axis in tenths. This means that exactly the same set of numbers can be used to draw very differently shaped lines.

Answers to self-tests

Test yourself: Part 1 (Chapter 1)

This is a tricky table because it does not give a very full explanation of the figures, and the percentages don't add up to 100%. However, we do have a row marked 'average' at the bottom, so we know that we should read the percentages horizontally – in other words, that in the Age Group rows, the numbers refer to a percentage of that age group.

1   10% of customers who bought books were aged 40–44 – *no*; 10% of customers aged 40–44 bought books, which is not the same thing.

2   10% of customers aged 40–44 bought books – *yes*.

3   Customers aged 40–44 were twice as likely to buy books as those aged 20–24 – *no*; they were half as likely.

Test yourself: Part 2 (Chapter 1)

What has happened is that the figures for holidays have included sleeping and meal times, which have already been counted, and the weekend figure includes weekends that occur in the holidays as well as sleeping and eating times. A childish ploy, you might think, but complicated forms of it crop up all the time in the adult world.

Test yourself: Part 3 (Chapter 1)

1   (a) is correct. (b) and (c) are true for normal distributions, but may not be true for other distributions.

2   You would look up the temperature records for London and Bath, and see how many times −6 occurred in London and −8 occurred in Bath. The one that occurred less frequently is the more extraordinary event.

3   The answer is (c). Half of the reports are between Q (1) and Q (3).

Test yourself: Part 4 (Chapter 2)

1   (b) is a more precise definition than (c), and (a) is wrong.

2   Your sample of 100 subscribers is not representative of your 35,000 subscribers because you did not select them at random. Also, we did not know whether or not the 35,000 subscribers to the magazine are representative of the 5 million early adopters. Because of poor sampling, the results of your survey are not representative of the views of the 5 million early adopters about which you are making a claim.

3   You have taken a representative sample of the population of cans with red labels, not of all the cans in the warehouse.

Test yourself: Part 5 (Chapter 2)

1   Year 1, because:

Year 1 = (93 − 81)/9 = 1.33
Year 2 = (93 − 78)/12 = 1.25

2   The answer is (a), 62 to 72 inches:

70 − (1.96 × 3) / 3, 70 + (1.96 × 3) / 3
70 − (5.88 / 3) = 1.96, so the range is plus or minus 2 inches from 70 inches.

Test yourself: Part 6 (Chapter 3)

1   The tip of the 40% slice does not reach the centre of the circle of the pie chart. This gives the visual impression that the slice is smaller than 40%.

2   By starting the vertical scale at £144,000, instead of 0, the chart exaggerates the price differences between the three years, which are actually only different by a fraction of 1%.

Test yourself: Part 7 (Chapter 5)

1   Not really. A random strategy is optimal, but in the long run would produce wins a third of the time, draws a third of the time and losses a third of the time.

2   Yes. Playing the same item every time would soon lead to losing every time.

3   Yes. If one player wins, the other loses.

Test Yourself: Part 8 (Chapter 6)

1   The methods people on a small income adopted. One of the main ways that people fought inflation was to try to acquire valuable objects, for example by bartering their services. If you could get hold of, say, a Harley Davidson motorbike or a pool table, it would retain its value as paper money inflated.

2   Listed companies pay regular dividends to their investors because ...? Some investors feel more comfortable if they see a regular return from a company because it makes the investment look more like a bond. However, dividends are heavily taxed in some countries, which makes them unattractive to investors who pay tax there.

3   Payback might not be an adequate method for comparing investment performance because ...? Payback tells you nothing about the long term prospects of the business. Suppose that a project with a 10-year payback turns out to generate a 10% real return for the next 100 years. That would be a very rewarding investment, but would be ruled out by a short termist payback threshold.

Glossary

Algorithm   A set of step-by-step instructions for performing a mathematical process or solving a problem.

Alternative hypothesis   In statistics, the hypothesis that describes the statement you hope that is true.

Amortisation   The process of paying off a loan in instalments.

APR   The Annual Percentage Rate, a rate of interest that includes the effective rate of interest combined with any commission charges and other fees.

APT (Arbitrage Pricing Theory)   A theory using several factors to measure stock market risk.

Annuity   Any transaction involving regular payments of money over time.

Arithmetic mean   The average obtained by adding a set of numbers together and dividing the result by the number of numbers in the set.

Average   A number used to represent the mid-point of a set of numbers; the three most common averages are the mean, the median and the mode.

Base   The number that is divided into all the other numbers to give an index of 1 or 100 is the base value of the index.

Base weighted index   An index of weighted averages where the weights do not change over time.

Bear   An individual who believes that a stock, future or option will go down in value.

Bernoulli variables   Variables which have two possible states, 'success' or 'failure'.

Beta risk   In the Capital Asset Pricing Model (CAPM), beta is the name for the value given to the risk of a stock.

Bias   In statistics, results which contain errors are said to have bias.

Binomial theorem   A statistical theorem that deals with data which have one of two outcomes.

Bull   An individual who believes that a stock, future or option will go up in value.

CAPM (Capital Asset Pricing Model)   A way of measuring the stock's risk relative to the overall stock market risk.

Categorical data   Information which is divided into categories.

Central Limit Theorem   A statistical theorem that the distributions of means of increasingly larger samples will tend towards a normal distribution.

Chaos theory   The search for predictable patterns in the charts of stock price movements.

Chi-squared test   A statistical test of goodness of fit.

Cluster sampling   A sampling method.

Coefficient   In the term 5x, 5 is the coefficient of x.

Collinearity   A set of points are collinear if they are on the same line.

Column player   In a two-person matrix in Game Theory, one person is arbitrarily chosen as the column player, and appears at the top of the payoff matrix.

Combined probabilities   The probability of two events occurring together.

Compound interest   Interest which is earned both on the sum originally invested and on any interest it subsequently earns.

Conditional probability   The probability that an event will occur given that another event has occurred.

Confidence   In statistics, the degree of accuracy of an estimate.

Confidence interval   The range of an estimate to a certain degree of confidence.

Constant   A value which is fixed in a particular situation. In the term 3x, 3 is a constant value, while x may change its value.

Conversion period   The period of time after which interest is calculated and added to the principal

Correlation   A relationship between two variables, measured on a scale between −1 and 1.

CPA (Critical path analysis)   A method of planning and estimating large projects.

Critical value   The value at which a hypothesis must be accepted or rejected.

Currency   Objects (such as coins and banknotes) that are used as a medium of exchange. The denomination of money of a particular country.

Current-weighted index   An index where weights change as time passes. Indexes of consumer prices are often current weighted.

Cycle   A repeating pattern of numbers.

Deciles   If a set of numbers is ranked in order and divided into ten equal parts, each tenth is a decile.

Decimal places   Numbers are often written with accuracy to a certain number of decimal places, which are counted to the right of the decimal point, e.g 2.561 is correct to three decimal places. 2.56 is correct to three decimal places.

Deduction   In statistics, the process of making an assumption about a subset of a population after analysing the whole population.

Degrees of freedom   In statistics, the number of observations minus 1.

Descriptive measures   Measures which describe distributions.

Deterministic   A problem which depends on certain parameters rather than probabilistic parameters.

Discounted cash flow   A method of converting all cash flows of different investments into a standard form to make appraisal easier.

Dispersion   In statistics, the way that a set of values are spread about the average.

Distribution   In statistics, a set of related values.

Diversification   In the stock market, a way of reducing risk by investing in a range of shares.

Dominance   In Game Theory, a row which the row player need never play because another row would be just as successful is said to be dominated by one of the column player's columns.

e   The number 2.71828 which is the base of 'natural' logarithms.

Effective interest rate   The interest rate when converted to one conversion period per year.

Efficient market theory   The theory that share prices adjust themselves almost instantaneously to news affecting them.

Equation   A set of terms with an 'equals' sign in the middle.

Exchange rate   The ratio at which one currency can be exchanged for another.

Exponent   The power of a number: 3 is the exponent of 2^3.

Exponential distribution   The distribution of constant growth over time.

Extrapolation   Making predictions by extending past trends into the future.

F-test   A statistical test that compares the variances of two normal distributions.

Factorial   The factorial of a number is found by multiplying all whole numbers from 1 up to and including the number. The symbol for factorial is !.

Feasible region   In linear programming, all the possible solutions to a problem are in the feasible region.

Foreign exchange   The process of buying the currency of one nation with the currency of another.

Fundamental analysis   The analysis of company information to arrive at an estimate of the value of its shares.

Future value   The sum of money obtained at a future point by investing money now at a given rate of interest.

Game theory   A theory of how opposing economic forces should behave in order to get optimum results.

Garch theory   A theory that there are predictable trends in the volatility of share prices.

Geometric mean   The geometric mean of given numbers is the square root of the product of the numbers multiplied together.

Goodness-of-fit test   Any statistical test which compares observations with probabilities to see how well the probabilities 'fit' the relative frequencies of the observations,

Hypothesis test   In statistics, the process of testing a theory about a population.

Index number   A value found by dividing a particular number by a base value is the index of that number.

Induction   In statistics, generalising about a population from the analysis of a sample.

Inequality   Symbols which denote relationships between numbers that are not equal.

Inference   The process of making assumptions about a population after analysing a sample.

Inflation   The economic process by which a currency's spending power decreases.

Intercept   On a graph, the intercept is where two lines cross.

Interquartile range   If a set of data is arranged in order, the one-quarter and three-quarter points are the upper and lower quartiles. The difference between them is the interquartile range.

Interval   The set of numbers which lie between two numbers.

Kruskal-Wallis test   A statistical test which compares two or more populations when the data are not normally distributed.

Linear programming   A way of solving a problem by finding the optimal solution.

Linear regression analysis   A technique of finding straight line relationships between sets of data.

Linear relationship   The tendency of a scattergram to form towards a line.

Logarithm   The power of a number: 2 is the log of 100 to base 10, since $10^2 = 100$.

Long wave (Kondratiev wave)   A theory that there is a 45- to 60-year cycle in the world economy.

Markov chain   A theory which describes a series of events which occur in stages over time.

Matrix   An array of numbers aligned in rows and columns in which the position of each number has special importance.

Maximisation   In game theory, the need for the row player to gain the maximum number from the payoff matrix.

Mean   The mean, or arithmetic mean, is the average of a set of numbers obtained by adding the numbers together and dividing by the number of numbers in the set.

Market risk   The average risk of the stock market as a whole.

Median   An average of a set of numbers which is the middle number when they are arranged in order of size.

Minimisation   In game theory, the need for the column player to gain the minimum number from the payoff matrix.

Mode   The most frequently occurring number in a set of numbers.

Modelling   Using the relationships between numbers to imitate real-life problems.

MPT (Modern Portfolio Theory)   A theory of reducing the risk of stock market investment by diversification.

Moving average   A series of values which are the means of values from a number of consecutive time periods.

Multiple   The number produced by multiplying other numbers together.

Natural logarithms   Logs to the base p.

NPV (net present value)   The present value of an investment minus the present value of outgoings.

Network analysis   The process of breaking down a project into its component tasks and estimating optimal workflows.

Neural network   Computer programs used in the stock market to find patterns in data.

Non-parametric method   Any statistical test that makes no assumptions about the parameters of a distribution.

Normal distribution   In statistics, a frequently occurring distribution which is a bell-shaped curve.

Null hypothesis   In statistics, the hypothesis that is to be tested. Usually the study hopes to show that this hypothesis is false.

Objective function   In linear programming, the relationship that is to be maximised or minimised.

Optimal solution   In game theory, the best solution for a player in a strictly determined game.

Outcome   In game theory, the result of a game.

Parameter   A measure of a population distribution.

Parametric method   A statistical test which makes assumptions about the parameters of a distribution.

Payback period   The time it takes to get back an investment.

Pay-off matrix   In game theory, the matrix that represents the possible outcomes for opposing players.

Percentage   A proportion expressed as a proportion of one hundred: 2 out of 10 is 20%.

Percentiles   When a set of observations are ordered in size and divided by 100, each hundredth part is a percentile.

Permutation   The name for rearranging a given group of items.

Pi π   The ratio between the circumference and the radius of a circle.

Pie chart   A circular chart divided to show the proportions that several categories take up of the whole circle.

Population   Any group of items about which generalisations are to be made using statistics.

Portfolio   Owning a number of different stocks is called owning a portfolio of stocks.

Power   If 1,000 is written as 10^3, 3 is the power, or index.

Present value   A way of calculating the amount necessary to invest now to generate a sum in the future at a given rate of interest.

PE ratio (price earnings ratio)   The ratio of a share price to its current earnings

Principal   In finance, the original sum of money that is invested.

Probability   The measure of the chance of an event occurring. A probability of 1 indicates the certainty, and a probability of 0 indicates the impossibility, of an event occurring.

Quartiles   If numbers in a set are arranged in order of size, the quarter points are the quartiles.

Queueing   The analysis of waiting in line.

r   The notation for a measure of correlation.

Random   The condition of being patternless or chaotic.

Range   The difference between the lowest and the highest figures in a set of data.

Rate of return   The percentage of profit earned on capital.

Raw data   In statistics, numerical information to which no process has yet been applied.

Regression analysis   A method of analysing the relationship between different series of data.

Residual   In regression analysis, the difference between actual values and estimated values are the residuals.

Row player   In a two-person matrix in game theory, one player is arbitrarily chosen as the row player, and appears on the left-hand side of the pay-off matrix.

Root   The opposite of a power: the 4th root of 16 is 2, since $2 \times 2 \times 2 \times 2 = 16$ $16^{1/4} = 2$.

Rounding   The name for writing a number correct to the nearest whole number or a given number of decimal places.

Saddle point   In game theory, a strictly determined 2×2 game which gives an optimal solution for both players.

Sample   The name in statistics for a subset of a population that is to be tested in order to make statements about the whole population.

Scalar   A number multiplied by a matrix.

Scattergram   A graph where observations are plotted as points.

Seasonal trend   In time series analysis, the name for a trend which regularly recurs in different periods of time.

Semi-interquartile range   If a set of data is arranged in order, the one quarter and three quarter points are the upper and lower quartiles. The difference between them is the interquartile range and half of it is the semi-interquartile range.

Serial correlation   In time series, the pairing of residuals in succession.

Significance test   In statistics, the probability of making the error of thinking something is the case when it is not.

Significant figures   The name for the most important figures in a number, for instance, 20,111 is written as 20,100 correct to three significant figures.

Simple interest   Interest which is paid on the original sum only and not on the interest subsequently earned.

Simplex algorithm   An algorithm for solving linear programming problems in non-geometric form.

Sinking fund   A fund into which deposits of money are made to save up to pay for the replacement of an asset which will wear out in the future, such as a car or a roof.

Skew   A distribution where most of the observations are clustered towards one end.

Spread   In a distribution, the spread is the range of values of the observations.

Spreadsheet   A table in computer software that can perform mathematical operations on the data entered.

Spurious correlation   When a cause and effect relationship is wrongly attributed to a correlation, it is called 'spurious'.

Standard deviation   A measure of dispersion; the distance from the mean is found for each number in the set, and then squared. The mean of the squares is found, called the variance. The standard deviation is the square root of the variance.

Standard error   The standard deviation of a statistic.

Statistics   The science of analysing data.

Statistical test   A method of analysing data.

Stratified sampling   A method of sampling by breaking down a population into categories.

Strictly determined   In game theory, a 2 × 2 game is strictly determined if there is an entry in the matrix which is simultaneously the minimum in its row and the maximum in its column.

Subset   A subset of the set of numbers (3,4, 5) is (3,4). Any subset has some of the members of the original set, or nothing at all (an empty set).

Summary measure   A measure of a population.

Superset   A set of numbers which includes all the numbers in another set is the superset of that set.

t-test   A statistical test for small samples. As the sample gets larger, the t distribution approaches the normal.

Table   An arrangement of numbers or letters in rows and columns.

Technical analysis   A theory of estimating future share prices on the basis of past movements.

Term $y - 1 - 2x + 3$ has three terms, y, 2x and 3.

Test statistic   A statistic calculated from sample data which is used to test the null hypothesis.

Time series   A series of measurements taken at different points in time, such as sales figures or output.

Transpose   The transpose of a matrix is where the rows and columns of a matrix are reversed.

Trend   A pattern in a time series.

Type 1 and Type 2 errors   In statistics, a Type I error is made when the null hypothesis is rejected although it is true, and a Type 2 error is made when the alternative hypothesis is rejected when it is true.

Value of a game   In a strictly determined game, the saddle point gives the value. The value is the payoff of a game.

Variable   A letter which is used to represent numbers which may vary.

Variance   A statistical measure of how a set of data is spread around its mean.

Waiting lines   In queueing, the lines of customers waiting for service.

Weighted average   An average where different elements are favoured differently to represent their relative importance.

Wilcoxon test   A statistical test which compares the ranked or qualitative data (which do not have a normal distribution).

Zero sum game   In game theory, a game in which one person's gains are wholly at the expense of the other player.

Index

Comprehensive. Authoritative. Trusted

9780273723967

9780273727873

9780273723745

9780273745822

9780273722014

9780273729846

9780273712671

9780273724520

9780273729105

9780273727835

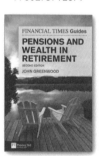

9780273763031

9780273729969

9780273736868

9780273761990

9780273756668

9780273735656

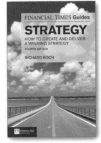
9780273745471

9780273738022

9780273742999

9780273734444

9780273756200

9780273750468

9780273743552

9780273730002

9780273751335

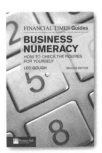
9780273746430

Change your business life today